My CUISINART® CLASSIC WAFFLE *Maker Cookbook*

101 CLASSIC AND CREATIVE BELGIAN WAFFLE RECIPES WITH INSTRUCTIONS

BY

TARA ADAMS

HHF PRESS
SAN FRANCISCO

Legal Notice

The information contained in this book is for entertainment purposes only. The content represents the opinion of the author and is based on the author's personal experience and observations. The author does not assume any liability whatsoever for the use of or inability to use any or all information contained in this book, and accepts no responsibility for any loss or damages of any kind that may be incurred by the reader as a result of actions arising from the use of information in this book. Use this information at your own risk.

The author reserves the right to make any changes he or she deems necessary to future versions of the publication to ensure its accuracy.

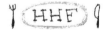

DO YOU LIKE FREE BOOKS?

Every month we release a new book, and we offer it to our current readers first...absolutely free! This helps us get early feedback before launching a book, and lets you stock your shelf full of interesting and valuable books for free!

Some recent titles include:

- The Complete Vegetable Spiralizer Cookbook
- My Lodge Cast Iron Skillet Cookbook
- 101 The New Crepes Cookbook

To receive this month's free book, just go to

http://www.healthyhappyfoodie.org/z1-freebooks

Table Of Contents

1

Why You Need This Book!

The ONLY Book Written for the Cuisinart Classic Waffle Maker

When it comes to making those amazing, fluffy, melt-in-your-mouth waffles with your Cuisinart Classic Waffle Maker—you need this book because there is no other book like it. You'll learn pro tips on how to make the perfect waffles every time, including delicious mouthwatering recipes and secrets from seasoned cooks and professional chefs that will keep you cooking the best waffles ever! This really is the ONLY book written for Cuisinart Classic Waffle Maker and the only book you'll need to whip up a delicious breakfast, afternoon snack, dessert or even dinner with scrumptious waffles.

Over 100 Mouthwatering Recipes

The best part about this book isn't the pro tips you'll get to make fluffy, perfect waffles over and over—it's the 101 mouthwatering recipes you'll get to try out with your Cuisinart Classic Waffle Maker. Not just for delicious waffles, your Cuisinart Classic Waffle Maker can be used to whip up Cinnamon Waffles, Cheesy Waffles, Pumpkin Waffles, BLT Waffles, Waffled Hash Browns—even Crab Cake Waffles! No matter what meal is your favorite one of the day, there's a waffle recipe you're sure to fall in love with when you start experimenting with the 101 scrumptious recipes in this book.

A Great Way to Make Healthy Breakfast, Desserts, and Snacks

When it comes to all the amazing 101 recipes you get in this book, you'll learn waffles aren't just for breakfast. Waffles are a great healthy way to whip up simple desserts, an afternoon snack to curb hunger cravings, and of course a great healthy breakfast that is quick and simple for anyone on the go. No matter what your lifestyle there are healthy ways to create waffles that accommodate any vegetarian, vegan, gluten-free, paleo, diabetic, and clean-eating lifestyle, You'll learn the best ways to get the most out of your Cuisinart Classic Waffle Maker and that all starts with healthy, scrumptious recipes!

"Street Wise" Pro Tips for Perfect Waffles

It's a no-brainer that you'll want to whip up the most deliciously decadent, flawless waffles every time you use your Cuisinart Classic Waffle Maker. That's why you'll get an entire chapter in this book dedicated to the art of the waffle that teaches you all those amazing "street wise" pro tips for the perfect waffle. From learning the best ingredients to use in your waffle batter to the best way to whip up the perfect batter, as well as storing your fresh waffles and how to reheat those yummy waffles—you'll get all those pro tips and more with this book.

Get More Out of Your Cuisinart Classic Waffle Maker!

Cuisinart Classic Waffles aren't just for breakfast. You'll learn how to create tantalizing desserts, mouthwatering lunch, and dinner, as well as delicious desserts and side dishes—all using your Cuisinart Classic Waffle Maker. Did we mention that your waffle recipes can be modified to create amazing clean-eating, gluten-free, diabetic-friendly, paleo, vegetarian, and vegan lifestyle recipes! You learn how to modify with ease to whip up the best waffles ever, no matter what your healthy lifestyle is.

The Only Waffle Book You'll Ever Need!

With all the comprehensive tips and tricks to get you cooking like a pro to the 101 mouthwatering recipes, this really is the ONLY waffle book you'll ever need. This book will also educate you on how to clean and store your Cuisinart Waffle Maker for years of waffle fun, and you'll even get a Bonus Chapter to teach you, even more, top tips and pro secrets on how to get the most out of your Cuisinart Waffle Maker.

2

Why Choose Cuisinart?

It Is the Easiest Way to Make Fluffy, Fresh, and Delicious Waffles Right at Home

This machine is so easy to use that the whole family can enjoy making waffles. A dual lighting system tells you when the machine is on and when it is ready to cook. It has 5 browning settings that work as a timer just like your toaster to make the perfectly soft or crisp waffles every time. The lid to this machine is weighted so there is no worry about the lid rising during cooking and interfering with consistency. The grid itself is made with non-stick material so you can easily transfer your perfect waffle from the machine to the plate while it is hot and ready to eat.

Cuisinart is Diet-friendly

Get healthy and eat clean with Cuisinart Classic Waffle Maker. Light, golden, fluffy waffles are just what you need to fuel the day, recover from a workout, curb hunger cravings, or whip a dinner that will keep you motivated on your healthy lifestyle journey. With this book for you'll learn exactly what to have on hand for your Cuisinart Classic Waffle Maker. All the tantalizing sauces & syrups you can use to highlight your scrumptious Cuisinart Classic Waffles and healthy lifestyle are also included in the Bonus Chapter. Along with non-dairy alternatives, gluten-free options, and paleo friendly toppings!

No Preservatives, GMOs, or Unhealthy Additives

With the Cuisinart Classic Waffle Maker, you'll whip up your own healthy batter right at home—so you know there are no preservatives, GMOs, or unhealthy additives. You'll get delicious and nutritious waffles every time you use your Cuisinart Classic Waffle Maker. Plus, you decide what types of toppings, sauces, syrups and fun additions you use to make your scrumptious waffles. You can modify each recipe to be cholesterol friendly, heart healthy, diabetic friendly or just plain nutritious and delicious. Because there are no preservatives, you'll also learn how to properly store your delicious Cuisinart Classic Waffles, for quick and easy reheating for the healthy waffle lover on the go.

A Quick and Easy Treat for Kids!

The Cuisinart Classic Waffle Maker is super-family friendly and great for little chefs! With the 101 mouthwatering recipes, you'll get loads of kid-friendly fun. Teach your kids about the proper handling of kitchen appliances with the Cuisinart Classic Waffle Maker. Turn a rainy day or snow day into endless waffle fun. Create nutritious and delicious after-school snacks for the kids with the easy to use Cuisinart Classic Waffle Maker. In this book, you'll learn just how quick and easy Cuisinart Classic Waffles really are!

3

A Brief History of the Waffle

Interesting Historical Timeline & Facts:

No one really knows where the waffle was born. In the beginning, the delicious, iconic honeycomb printed, fluffy waffle began as a simple, flat cake. Some believe them to be born from obelios, a flat cake cooked in between hot metal plates from ancient Greece.

As the popularity of obelios spread throughout medieval Europe, the cakes then made from a mixture of flour, water or milk, and sometimes eggs became known as wafers where the Europeans began to cook them over an open fire between iron plates with long handles. During the 13th century, the wafer was seen stamped with designs ranging from family crests to landscape scenes, as well as the characteristic grid or honeycombed pattern you see today.

As history would have it, the Dutch were particularly fond of "wafles" and passed their love of the delicious cake onto those headed to the New World. Colonists soon brought the fluffy, golden cakes to the New World in the early 17th century—thanks to none other than Thomas Jefferson. He was rumored to have brought the first long-handled waffle iron to America in 1789. It was in the New World where the waffle met it's soon to be age old mate maple syrup. By 1735, the confectionary treat was entered into the English language with an extra "f" as we know it to be spelled today.

80 years later, New York's Cornelius Swarthout patented the first stovetop waffle iron. Waffle cones for ice cream then followed with a debut at the 1904 World's Fair in St. Louis. As the industrial revolution swept across America, the old stovetop waffle irons were outfitted for electricity and became common household appliances by the 1930s. It was only in 1962, that the bigger, thicker, more yeast-leavened Belgian Waffle made its way to the Americas; making its beloved debut at the Seattle World's Fair.

Difference Between the Waffle Maker and Waffle Iron

Simply put—A waffle iron is for stove top or open campfire use. Usually made of cast-iron for a non-stick quality once seasoned. The stove or campfire heats the waffle iron in order to create the fluffy waffles. A waffle maker is a kitchen appliance that requires electricity in order to heat it for cooking waffles. Waffle irons are also usually square in nature and tend to render thinner waffles. Waffle makers tend to make more cake-like waffles with that Belgian waffle quality.

Why Cuisinart Classic is the Best Waffle Maker

There are so many features that make this machine so wonderful that it is hard to know where to begin. Of course, the main benefit of this waffle maker is that it makes the perfect waffle every time. It has a 5 level browning switch that is so easy to use that you can literally move it with a finger. Being able to choose the doneness of the waffle that easily, means that you make waffles for the entire family in one sitting no matter how picky your family is. Dual indicator lights let you know when the machine is on and when it is ready to bake so there is never any problems with adding the batter too soon. The non-stick grid plates on the inside make transferring cooked waffles easy and clean-up is a breeze. The stainless steel exterior also lends itself to easy clean-up making this device just as easy to clean as it is to cook with. Lastly, there is not an easier to store waffle maker on the market today. With a smart cord design and the fact that it can be stored vertically there is no way that you can't find a spot for this machine.

Waffles from Around the World
and How to Prepare Them

While a Brussels waffle doesn't need any other garnish than a simple dusting of powdered sugar. This sweet waffle is also commonly served with a topping of chocolate sauce, fruit and/or whipped cream—especially in America.

In Italy, the waffle is also known as pizzelle. A waffle cookie, it's made with a batter that is flavored with vanilla, star anise, or lemon zest. The pizzelle iron is made with its very own decorative pattern. The gorgeous flat, crisp cookie is sometimes dusted with sugar.

The Hong Kong waffle also known as grid cakes are very similar to the classic waffle. A Hong Kong waffle is round in shape and divided into four quarters. The soft waffle is then served as hot street food, with peanut butter and sugar spread on one side. In order to eat them, you fold them double.

In Scandinavia, they make their waffles adorably sweet and totally heart-shaped. Often topped with a wide range of sweet or scrumptiously savory things, the waffle is loved here. Popular toppings include whipped cream, sometimes sour cream, jams, berries, sugar, ice cream, and salmon and cheese.

4

How to Use Your Cuisinart Classic Waffle Maker

Detailed Instructions on Using Your Cuisinart Classic Waffle Maker

- Place the waffle maker on a flat, heat resistant, surface.
- Before using your waffle maker for the first time, wipe it down with a damp cloth to remove any dust or debris.
- Plug the machine in and allow it to preheat; the red indicator light will let you know that the machine is being powered and the green indicator light will turn on when the machine is preheated.
- While your waffle maker preheats, mix your batter according to your recipe.

- When the green light indicates that you are ready, pour the batter mix into the bottom grid and use a heat proof spatula to spread it around so it is even.
- Set your browning level by sliding the switch at the bottom of the machine and close the lid.
- When you close the weighted lid you will see the green light turn off and the red light turn on. The green light will again turn on when the waffles are ready to eat.
- When you are ready to remove the waffle from the machine use a heat proof plastic spatula or tongs to transfer the waffle. Never use metal utensils to remove the waffle as you could damage the non-stick coating on the grid plate.

How to Clean and Store
Your Cuisinart Classic Waffle Maker

One of the biggest benefits of this waffle maker is how easy it is to clean. That is of the utmost importance when you have a busy family.

The first and most important step when cleaning your waffle maker is to make sure that it is unplugged and cooled down before you clean it.

Never use any kind of abrasive cleaning products including sprays and sponges, they can ruin the cooking grid and scratch the stainless steel outer surface.

Use a damp cloth to wipe the outside of the machine along with the cord.

A damp cloth should also suffice for wiping down the inside of the machine; if there is any baked on batter drip a few drops of cooking oil on it and let it sit for a few minutes to soften the batter, then wipe it away.

Allow the machine to air dry before storage.

When you are ready to store the machine you can wrap the cord around the bottom.

This waffle maker is specifically designed to be stored vertically to save space, simply place it on its opening end in the shelf and you will have plenty of room for other appliances.

5

Pro Tips To Make Perfect Waffles

Make Perfectly Fluffy Waffles Every Time

Use a rubber spatula or a spoon to slowly and carefully mix the wet ingredients of your batter into the dry ingredients. Using a gentle motion and a couple extra minutes, mix the batter until smooth.

You'll want to use a 3/4 cups batter in the deep-pocket 7″ Cuisinart Classic Waffle Maker. This should be enough batter to completely cover the surface of the iron and will make a perfectly round waffle every time. If you find the batter is thinned, simply pour up to 1 cup into the waffle maker.

How to Store Your Fresh Waffles

Storing your fresh cooked Cuisinart waffles has never been so easy. Simply refrigerate within two hours of cooking. You'll want to cover your Cuisinart waffles with foil or plastic wrap, then place in plastic bag to prevent drying out. Refrigerated waffles are great for 7 days.

In order to freeze Cuisinart Classic waffles, just place a sheet of wax paper between each waffle, then wrap waffles super tight in plastic wrap or aluminum foil and place in heavy-duty freezer bag. Frozen waffles can be kept up to 2 to 4 weeks if sealed properly.

Best Way to Reheat Waffles

To reheat your Cuisinart Classic Waffles, simple place in a bagel toaster or toaster oven and heat through one toaster cycle. The waffle may need two cycles depending on thickness. Test inner warmth with a toothpick or fork. Alternatively, waffles can be reheated in an oven at 350 degrees Fahrenheit for 10-15 minutes.

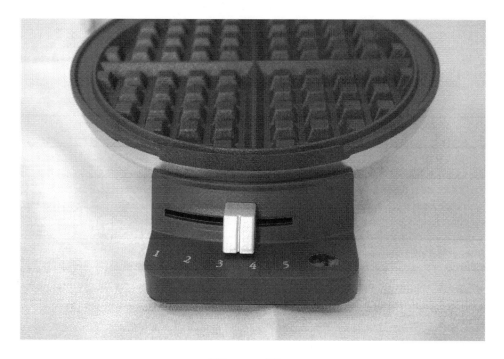

Timer Tips

In the case of the Cuisinart Classic Waffle Maker there is not a traditional timer, but instead a browner which works as a timer. You can choose to use an outside timer if you would like but it really isn't necessary.

When you get into using a plethora of different batters your time will depend on how long it takes each type of batter to set up. The timer has no reflection on if the waffle is done.

Waffles have a natural kitchen timer: steam. If you don't like the timer, don't set it. Simply watch the iron quit steaming. When no steam rises out of the Cuisinart Classic Waffle Maker, your waffle is done!

Alternatively, you should experiment with your Cuisinart waffles. Check them at 2-3 minutes in. If the waffle is not done, cook 30 seconds longer and check again. While the instruction booklet may instruct a cooking time of 4 minutes, this usually results in burnt waffles. Three minutes 45 seconds is normally the longest cook time you will use.

How to Get the Most Out of Your Batter

Preheat the Cuisinart Classic Waffle Maker for several minutes. I recommend preparing the batter while you wait for the waffle maker to come to temperature and the indicator light goes out.

Don't overfill with batter. This can alter the cooking time and cause the waffle to be golden, yet doughy on the inside.

Be sure to spray both sides of the waffle maker with non-stick cooking spray before pouring in the batter. This helps slide the waffle right out of the Cuisinart Classic Waffle Maker and makes for easy cleanup!

Some chefs believe the non-stick is in the batter. If you find your waffles always stick, try adding a little more oil or butter to your batter recipe.

For super fluffy and light waffles, separate the egg yolks from the whites. Beat the yolks in a small mixing bowl. Add the beaten yolks to the wet ingredients of your batter. Next, beat the egg whites until stiff peaks form. Fold the eggs whites gently into the final batter using an icing spatula.

Avoid mixing the waffle batter violently. Waffle batter can be very tricky. The consistency should be smooth enough to flow freely through the dimples of the waffle plate. Over-mixing turns the flour into gluten which produces a chewy, non-fluffy texture.

No Buttermilk? Have no worries. A lot of the more complex waffle recipes call for buttermilk. If you can't find buttermilk or have none lying around, regular milk can be used in place of buttermilk. Mix up a substitute by adding one tablespoon of vinegar or lemon juice to one cup of milk. The acidic ingredient will cause the milk to curdle. Let it stand 15 minutes and voila!

Keeping Waffles Warm While Cooking

Each recipe usually yields around 3 to 4 waffles each, so you'll want to keep the other waffles warm as you cook the remaining batter up. Simply, preheat an oven to warm or 200 degrees Fahrenheit. As you finish each Cuisinart waffle, immediately place each waffle directly on the oven rack. This will keep them warm and they will not get soggy while you cook up the rest of the batter.

6

Breakfast Waffles

Banana Waffles

Servings: 4 | Prep Time: 10 minutes | Cook Time: 5 minutes

Start the day with something different and whip up these yummy Banana Waffles for breakfast. Serve them up alongside Greek yogurt and honey for one decadently different breakfast with a whole lot of love.

Ingredients

4 tablespoons unsalted butter, melted

1 cup plus 2 tablespoons milk

1 teaspoon pure vanilla extract

2 cups all-purpose flour

1 tablespoon dark brown sugar, packed

1 1/2 teaspoons yeast

1/2 teaspoon salt

1/2 teaspoon ground cinnamon

1/4 teaspoon ground nutmeg

1/8 teaspoon ground ginger

Pinch of ground clove

2 eggs

3 whole ripe bananas, peeled and mashed

2 tablespoons Greek yogurt or kefir

Non-stick cooking spray

Greek yogurt, for topping
Honey, for drizzling

Instructions

1. Lightly beat two eggs in a small mixing bowl and set aside.

2. Whisk together the butter, vanilla and milk in a small mixing bowl. Set aside to rest and come to room temperature.

3. Sift together the flour, brown sugar, yeast, salt and spices in a large mixing bowl.

4. Whisk the wet ingredients into the dry ingredients until smooth.

5.   Fold in the beaten eggs. Cover the bowl loosely with plastic wrap and refrigerate for at least 12 hours, but up to 24.

6.   Thirty minutes before you want to make waffles, take the batter out of the refrigerator and allow it to come to room temperature.

7.   Stir the Greek yogurt into the mashed bananas. Fold the banana mixture into the batter until thoroughly combined.

8.   Preheat the waffle maker.

9.   Grease both sides of the waffle maker.

10. Cook 3 - 4 minutes or until golden brown; repeat until all waffles are cooked.

11. Serve with a dollop of Greek yogurt and drizzle with honey.

Nutritional Info: Calories: 493 | Sodium: 441 mg | Dietary Fiber: 4.5 g | Total Fat:16.1 g | Total Carbs: 74.9 g | Protein: 13.3 g.

Belgian Waffle

Servings: 8 | Prep Time: 15 minutes | Cook Time: 20 minutes

Serve up delicious, golden Belgian Waffles for breakfast with this scrumptious, easy recipe. Belgian waffles are great on their own or served with butter, warm syrup, or fresh fruit.

Ingredients:

1 package active dry yeast

4 cups all-purpose flour

1/4 cup and 2 3/4 cups milk, warmed

3 eggs, separated

3/4 cups butter, melted

1/2 cup white sugar or sugar substitute

1 1/2 teaspoons salt

2 teaspoons pure vanilla extract

Instructions

1. Dissolve yeast in 1/4 cup warm milk in a small mixing bowl. Let stand until creamy, about 10 minutes.

2. Whisk the egg yolks in a large mixing bowl. Fold in another 1/4 cup of the warm milk and the melted butter and whisk until just blended.

3. Whisk the yeast mixture, sugar, salt and vanilla into the egg yolks.

4. Alternate stirring in the flour and the remaining 2 1/2 cups of warm milk ending with the flour.

5. Beat the egg whites in a separate mixing bowl until they form soft peaks. Fold the egg whites into the batter.

6. Cover the bowl tightly with plastic wrap. Let rise in a warm place, for about 1 hour, until doubled in volume.

7. Pour one 1/2 cup batter into center of the waffle maker.

8.   Cook for 2 - 4 minutes or until golden and fluffy; repeat until batter is gone.

9.   Top with your favorite toppings and enjoy!

Nutritional Info: Calories: 498 | Sodium: 625 mg | Dietary Fiber: 1.9 g | Total Fat: 21.3 g | Total Carbs: 64.9 g | Protein: 11.8 g.

Blueberry Muffin Waffles

Servings: 2 - 4 | Prep Time: 5 minutes | Cook Time: 10 minutes

Turn your favorite morning muffin into a waffled masterpiece! Grab one to go with a protein smoothie or serve them up for the whole family to enjoy.

Ingredients

1/2 cup vegetable oil

1 cup ultra-filtered whole milk, like Fair Life

2 eggs

1 cup sugar or 1/2 cup sugar substitute

1 3/4 cups flour

1 teaspoon baking powder

1 cup blueberries, fresh or frozen

Non-stick cooking spray

Butter, for topping

Syrup, for topping

Instructions

1. Preheat the waffle maker.
2. In a large mixing bowl, whisk together the oil, milk, eggs, and sugar.
3. Add the flour and baking powder and whisk until well combined. Fold in the blueberries.
4. Fill the waffle iron with 3/4 cups of batter.
5. Cook for 2 - 3 minutes or until golden and fluffy. Transfer to a plate and carefully wipe off any blueberries that stuck to the iron before adding more batter for your next waffle; cook the remaining batter.
6. Serve with a pat of butter and your favorite syrup.

Nutritional Info: Calories: 717 | Sodium: 58 mg | Dietary Fiber: 2.4 g | Total Fat:32.1 g | Total Carbs: 100.5 g | Protein: 10.7 g.

Brownie Batter Waffles

Servings: 2 - 4 | Prep Time: 5 minutes | Cook Time: 10 minutes

Nothing quite hits the sweet spot like serving up Brownie Batter Waffles for breakfast. Absolutely delicious and covered in strawberry syrup, these waffles are a great addition to any brunch menu or breakfast for dinner too!

Ingredients

1/2 cup of flour

1/2 cup of cocoa powder

1/2 cup of almond meal

1 teaspoon baking powder

1/2 teaspoon salt

2 eggs

1/4 cup of sugar

1/4 cup of coconut oil, melted,

1 teaspoon vanilla

1/2 cup of milk

Crème fraiche, for topping

Fresh berries, for topping

Instructions

1. Combine the flour, cocoa, almond meal, salt and baking powder in a large mixing bowl.

2. In a separate mixing bowl whisk together the eggs and sugar.

3. Add in the oil and vanilla.

4. Gradually fold in the dry ingredients. Gradually fold in the milk.

5. Pour 1/4 cup batter into the waffle maker. Cook for 4 minutes and transfer to a plate.

6. Top with crème fraiche and fresh berries to serve.

Nutritional Info: Calories: 365 | Sodium: 340mg | Dietary Fiber: 5.1 g | Total Fat:23.9 g | Total Carbs: 35.3 g | Protein: 9.8 g.

Buttermilk Waffles

Servings: 4 - 6 | Prep Time: 5 minutes | Cook Time: 10 minutes

These delightfully crisp on the outside, light and fluffy on the inside waffles so delicious. Serve topped with a lot of butter and syrup for a classic waffle breakfast everyone will enjoy!

Ingredients

1 3/4 cups all-purpose flour

1 1/2 teaspoons baking powder

1 teaspoon baking soda

1/2 teaspoon sea salt

3 large eggs, separated

1/2 cup unsalted butter, melted and slightly cooled

1/3 cup granulated sugar

1 3/4 cups buttermilk

1 teaspoon pure vanilla extract

Butter, for topping

Syrup, for topping

Instructions

1. Preheat the waffle maker.

2. Preheat oven to 200F degrees. Place a wire rack on a baking sheet and set aside.

3. In a large mixing bowl, combine the flour, baking powder, baking soda, and salt; set aside.

4. In another large mixing bowl, whisk the egg yolks, butter, sugar, buttermilk, and vanilla together until combined.

5. Fold the wet ingredients into the dry ingredients and whisk gently until smooth; do not overmix.

6. In a medium mixing bowl, whisk the egg whites until stiff peaks form and gently fold the egg whites into the batter.

7. Pour 1/3 cup of the batter into the waffle maker.

8. Cook the waffle for 3 - 5 minutes or until the steam has ceased and waffle is golden brown.

9. Transfer the cooked waffles to the wire rack and keep warm in the preheated oven as you cook the rest; repeat to cook the remaining batter.

10. Serve the waffles warm with plenty of butter and maple syrup!

Nutritional Info: Calories: 378 | Sodium: 588 | Dietary Fiber: 1.0 g | Total Fat: 18.8 g | Total Carbs: 43.2 g | Protein: 9.4 g.

Chocolate Chip Waffle

Servings: 2 - 4 | Prep Time: 10 minutes | Cook Time: 15 minutes

Stuff your waffle with decadent chocolate chips for one super-sweet breakfast treat. Chocolate chip waffles are delicious when simply topped with butter and whipped cream, so you get an explosion of chocolate chips with every sweet bite!

Ingredients

1/2 cup light brown sugar

1/4 cup granulated sugar

1/2 cup butter

1 egg

1 teaspoon pure vanilla extract

1 cup all-purpose flour

1/4 cup milk

1/2 teaspoon salt

1/4 teaspoon baking soda

1/2 cup semi-sweet chocolate chips

Non-stick cooking spray

Butter, for topping

Whipped cream, for topping

Instructions

1. Melt the butter in a saucepan on low-medium heat.
2. Pour it into a large mixing bowl and add both sugars. Stir together until smooth.
3. Add milk, egg and vanilla; stir again until well-blended.
4. In a separate mixing bowl, whisk together the flour, soda and salt.
5. Fold the dry ingredients into the wet ingredients and mix well.
6. Fold the chocolate chips into the batter.
7. Scoop 1/4 cup batter into the waffle maker.

8. Cook for 2 - 3 minutes.

9. Remove and top with butter and whipped cream to serve.

Nutritional Info: Calories: 589 | Sodium: 654 | Dietary Fiber: 1.8 g | Total Fat: 31.6 g | Total Carbs: 71.9 g | Protein: 6.4 g.

Cinnamon Waffles

Servings: 4 | Prep Time: 15 minutes | Cook Time: 23 minutes

If you love cinnamon rolls, you'll fall in love with these sinfully sweet breakfast treats. Not just for breakfast, these delectable waffles can be served as a decadent dessert with a scoop of praline ice cream.

Ingredients

2 1/2 cups flour

2 tablespoons sugar

1 1/4 teaspoon baking powder

1/2 teaspoon baking soda

1/2 teaspoon salt

1 1/4 cups buttermilk

3 tablespoons unsalted butter, melted

For the Filling:

2/3 cups brown sugar

1 tablespoon cinnamon

1/8 teaspoon salt

2 tablespoons butter, melted

For the Icing:

2/3 cups powdered sugar

2 teaspoons unsalted butter, melted

1/4 teaspoon almond extract

2 teaspoons buttermilk

Instructions

1.   Whisk together flour, sugar, baking powder, soda, and salt in a large mixing bowl.

2. In a separate mixing bowl, combine the buttermilk and melted butter.

3. Whisk butter mix into the dry ingredients. Stir lightly until just combined.

4. Generously flour a workspace or large countertop. Roll dough into a rectangle that is about 12" x 9".

5. Combine all the filling ingredients in a small bowl until well-blended. Spread evenly over the dough.

6. Roll up, like a log, lengthwise and pinch ends to seal the seam.

7. Cut into 2-3" slices.

8. Preheat the waffle maker and grease.

9. Place a round into each of the four grids of the waffle maker. Set the timer for 2 minutes.

10. Cook until golden brown; repeat until all waffles are cooked.

11. Whisk together the icing ingredients until well-blended. Drizzle over the hot waffles and serve.

Nutritional Info: Calories: 177 | Sodium: 659 mg | Dietary Fiber: 3.0 g | Total Fat:17.8 g | Total Carbs: 115.2 g | Protein: 10.9 g.

Coffee Waffles

Servings: 1 | Prep Time: 5 minutes | Cook Time: 10 minutes

For the coffee lover—Coffee Waffles! If you love the rich, bold aroma of a fresh cup of joe then this waffle is just for you! Top with whipped cream or enjoy all on its own for that just brewed taste.

Ingredients

1 3/4 cups all-purpose flour

1/4 cup sugar or sugar substitute

1 teaspoon baking soda

1/2 teaspoon sea salt

1 1/2 cups milk

1/3 cup vegetable oil

1 large egg

1 teaspoon pure vanilla extract

1 tablespoon instant coffee

Non-stick cooking spray

Whipped cream, optional

Instructions

1. Mix together flour, sugar, baking soda and salt in a large mixing bowl.

2. In a medium mixing bowl, whisk milk, vegetable oil, egg, vanilla and instant coffee.

3. Add milk mixture to dry ingredients and whisk until just combined.

4. Spray waffle iron lightly with non-stick cooking spray.

5. Pour one 1/2 cup batter onto the waffle maker.

6. Cook until golden and fluffy, about 3 minutes.

7. Transfer to a plate and tent with aluminum foil to keep warm.

8.   Continue to cook batter until all waffles are cooked. Serve with whipped cream and enjoy.

Nutritional Info: Calories: 1893 | Sodium: 2442 | Dietary Fiber: 5.9 g | Total Fat: 87.3 g | Total Carbs: 235.8 g | Protein: 40.9 g.

Creamy Coconut Citrus Waffle

Servings: 1 | Prep Time: 5 minutes | Cook Time: 10 minutes

If you love a sublimely sweet breakfast, the Creamy Coconut Citrus Waffle is just the recipe for you. Loaded with sweet orange citrus and decadent coconut - this recipe might just knock your breakfast socks off!

Ingredients

2 waffles, from your favorite recipe above

1 tablespoon cream cheese

1/4 cup orange slices

2 teaspoons chopped unsalted macadamia nuts

2 teaspoons maple syrup

1 tablespoon toasted flaked sweetened coconut

Instructions

1. Lay your fresh cooked waffle onto a plate.
2. Add a dollop of cream cheese, top with orange sections, macadamia nuts, maple syrup, and coconut.
3. Simply enjoy!

Nutritional Info: Calories: 339 | Sodium: 392 | Dietary Fiber: 2.0 g | Total Fat: 16.5 g | Total Carbs: 43.0 g | Protein: 5.8 g.

Crispy Belgian Waffle

Servings: 4 | Prep time: 5 minutes | Cook time: 5 minutes

Serve up some crispy sweet waffles for breakfast with the Cuisinart Belgian Waffle Maker. Simple, easy and sweet—this recipe is so quick and easy you'll love making these even when you're on the go!

Ingredients

2 egg yolks, lightly beaten

2 cups milk

2 cups all-purpose flour

1 tablespoon baking powder

1/2 teaspoon salt

1/3 cup oil, and some for brushing

2 egg whites, stiffly beaten

Instructions

1. Whisk the egg yolks in a large mixing bowl. Fold in the milk and oil, and whisk until just blended.

2. Fold in the flour, baking powder and salt.

3. Beat the egg whites in a separate mixing bowl until they form soft peaks. Fold the egg whites into the batter.

4. Preheat the waffle maker.

5. Brush with oil and spoon about one 1/2 cup into center of the waffle maker.

6. Cook for 3-4 minutes or until golden and fluffy; repeat until batter is finished and all waffles are cooked.

7. Top with your favorite toppings or enjoy on their own as a crunchy snack.

Nutritional Info: Calories: 488 | Sodium: 374 | Dietary Fiber: 1.8 g | Total Fat: 23.6 g | Total Carbs: 55.9 g | Protein: 13.6 g.

Eggs Benedict Waffles

Servings: 4 | Prep time: 10 minutes | Cook time: 30 minutes

A twist on the traditional dish, this recipe combines the best of both breakfast worlds for a sweet and savory meal that is out of this world. When you serve these up—don't forget the mimosas!

Ingredients

For the Waffles:

3 eggs

3/4 cups raw cashew butter-like Artisana

3 tablespoons ultra-filtered milk, like Fair Life

2 teaspoons bacon fat, melted

3/4 teaspoons minced garlic

1/4 teaspoon sea salt

3/4 teaspoons baking soda

3 tablespoons coconut flour

1 piece of bacon, cooked and roughly chopped

2 chives, chopped

For the Benedict

4 savory waffles

4 slices cooked ham

4 eggs, poached

For the Hollandaise Sauce:

2 egg yolks

1/4 cup melted grass fed butter, like KerryGold

2 teaspoons lemon juice

1/4 teaspoon salt

1/8 teaspoon paprika, or cayenne if you like a little heat

Instructions

1. Preheat the waffle maker.
2. Use a handheld electric mixer to beat the eggs with the cashew butter, almond milk, bacon fat, and garlic in a large mixing bowl.
3. Mix the salt, baking soda and coconut flour in a small mixing bowl, then mix the dry ingredients into the wet mixture.
4. Beat for 30 seconds until the batter is fully incorporated; scrape the bottom of the bowl with the beater to make sure you get all of the sticky cashew butter incorporated.
5. Fold the chopped bacon and chives into the batter with a wooden spoon.
6. Scoop 3/4 cups batter into the waffle maker.
7. Cook until golden and fluffy, about 3 minutes. Transfer to a plate and tent with aluminum foil to keep warm.
8. Continue to cook batter until all waffles are cooked.

For the Hollandaise Sauce:

9. Pour boiling water into a blender, then cover and let sit for 10 minutes. Dump out the water and dry the container thoroughly. Blend the egg yolks with the lemon juice, salt, and paprika. With the blender running on low, slowly pour in the hot melted butter. Blend for about 30 seconds until the sauce has thickened and the butter is well incorporated. The sauce will continue to thicken as it cools.
10. Layer each waffle with a slice of ham, poached egg, drizzle of hollandaise, and a few chives.

Nutritional Info: Calories: 625 | Sodium: 1338 | Dietary Fiber: 0.6 g | Total Fat: 59.2 g | Total Carbs: 7.3 g | Protein: 17.7 g.

French Toast

Servings: 2 | Prep Time: 10 minutes | Cook Time: 10 minutes

Go bold for breakfast with this yummy brioche French Toast that is absolutely to die for! Turn breakfast or brunch into a decadent feast and serve up something sinfully sweet to kick start your day.

Ingredients

4 thick slices of brioche bread

1 egg

1 teaspoon ground cinnamon

1/2 teaspoon pure vanilla extract

1/2 cup ultra-filtered whole milk, like Fair Life

For the Topping:

2 tablespoons unsalted butter, melted

1/3 cup caster sugar

2 teaspoons ground cinnamon

Non-stick cooking spray

Instructions

1. Preheat the waffle maker.

2. In a wide, shallow dish place the egg, ground cinnamon and vanilla extract.

3. Whisk together well then pour in the milk and whisk in.

4. Dip a slice of brioche into the batter, turning to coat, then place into the waffle iron. Repeat with another slice of brioche.

5. Coat both sides of the waffle griddle with non-stick cooking spray.

6. Cook 3 - 4 minutes or until golden brown; repeat with the rest of the bread.

7. Combine the sugar and ground cinnamon in a small mixing bowl.

8. Brush the slices of cooked French toast with melted butter, and sprinkle generously with the cinnamon sugar to serve.

Nutritional Info: Calories: 655 | Sodium: 137 mg | Dietary Fiber: 1.8 g | Total Fat:24.7 g | Total Carbs: 97.2 g | Protein: 13.0 g.

French Toast Waffle

Servings: 4 | Prep Time: 15 minutes | Cook Time: 23 minutes

French toast lovers unite! This scrumptious recipe combines the best of both breakfast worlds for one very sweet treat. Start your morning off right by turning your Cuisinart Belgian Waffle Maker into breakfast heaven.

Ingredients

1 cup half and half

1 large egg

1/4 teaspoon ground cinnamon

1/8 teaspoon freshly grated nutmeg

4 slices potato bread

Butter, for topping

Maple syrup, for topping

Instructions

1. Whisk together the half and half, egg, cinnamon and nutmeg in a large mixing bowl; until well-blended.

2. Submerge one slice of bread in the egg mixture until well-coated. Let it soak in, then move the bread to the waffle iron.

3. Cook until the waffle iron timer goes off or steam no longer rises from the waffle iron.

4. Repeat with remaining bread slices until all the French Toast Waffles are cooked.

5. Serve with butter and syrup!

Nutritional Info: Calories: 177 | Sodium: 212 mg | Dietary Fiber: 0.8 g | Total Fat: 9.2 g | Total Carbs: 18.8 g | Protein: 6.4 g.

Gingerbread Waffles

Servings: 2 | Prep Time: 5 minutes | Cook Time: 10 minutes

Get creative with your Cuisinart Belgian Waffle Maker and serve up some waffles that are sure to warm your heart. Great for the winter months or holiday season, these tasty waffles are best served simple - with a lot of syrup and a cup of hot chocolate.

Ingredients

1 cup spelt flour

1 tablespoon ground flax seeds

2 teaspoons baking powder

1/4 teaspoon baking soda

1/4 teaspoon sea salt

1 teaspoon ground cinnamon

2 teaspoons ground ginger

1/4 cup brown sugar

1 1/4 cups non-dairy milk, like Almond or Coconut

1 tablespoon apple cider vinegar

2 tablespoons blackstrap molasses

1 1/2 tablespoons olive oil

Instructions

1. Grease and preheat the Cuisinart Belgian Waffle Maker.

2. Add all of the dry ingredients to a large mixing bowl and stir well.

3. In a separate mixing bowl, combine wet ingredients and stir until well-combined.

4. Fold the wet ingredients into the dry ingredients with a spoon, until just combined; do not over mix.

5.   Cook for 2 - 3 minutes or until dark golden and fluffy; repeat with remaining batter.

6.   Serve immediately covered in your favorite syrup.

Nutritional Info: Calories: 531 | Sodium: 487 | Dietary Fiber: 9.2 g | Total Fat: 16.0 g | Total Carbs: 89.4 g | Protein: 14.1 g.

Gluten-Free Low Carb Waffle

Servings: 4 - 6 | Prep Time: 10 minutes | Cook Time: 15 minutes

For the gluten-free dieter, this is the most sinfully sweet waffle on earth. Packed full of protein for some serious "get up and go", this waffle makes for one seriously healthy breakfast option.

Ingredients

2 eggs, large

1 teaspoon pure vanilla extract

2 tablespoons coconut oil, partially melted

1 1/2 cups almond milk

1 cup gluten-free flour blend

1 cup ground oat flour

2 teaspoons baking powder

1/2 teaspoon baking soda

2 scoops Vanilla Protein Powder

1/2 cup dairy-free chocolate chips

Non-stick cooking spray

Instructions

1. Preheat your Cuisinart Belgian Waffle Maker and lightly grease with non-stick cooking spray.
2. Place dry ingredients into a large mixing bowl and combine.
3. Add in the wet ingredients and mix until well-combined.
4. Pour 1/2 cup of batter into the waffle maker; spread evenly.
5. Cook for about 2-3 minutes or until golden and fluffy.
6. Serve with almond butter or fresh fruit.

Nutritional Info: Calories: 679 | Sodium: 250 | Dietary Fiber: 5.8 g | Total Fat: 39.4 g | Total Carbs: 60.4 g | Protein: 23.7 g.

Gritty Waffles

Servings: 4 | Prep Time: 15 minutes | Cook Time: 10 minutes

If you love cornbread, you'll love these gritty waffles. Rich and decadent, this recipe is best served with butter and syrup for a twist on the classic waffle. For a full meal, enjoy with a serving of bacon and a glass of orange juice on the side.

Ingredients

1/3 cup vegetable oil

1 cup cornmeal

1 cup all-purpose flour

1 1/2 teaspoons baking powder

1/2 teaspoon baking soda

1/4 teaspoon sea salt

2 large eggs, lightly beaten

2 cups buttermilk

Non-stick cooking spray

Instructions

1. Preheat and lightly grease the Cuisinart Belgian Waffle Maker with non-stick cooking spray.

2. Combine dry ingredients in a large mixing bowl and set aside.

3. Mix vegetable oil, buttermilk, and eggs in a separate mixing bowl.

4. Fold wet ingredients into the dry ingredients until a smooth batter forms; do not overmix.

5. Pour approximately 3/4 to 1 cup of waffle batter into the center of the bottom waffle grid until covered, but not leaking over the side.

6. Cook for 2 - 3 minutes. Top with your favorite butter and syrup.

Nutritional Info: Calories: 471 | Sodium: 452 | Dietary Fiber: 3.1 g | Total Fat: 23.1 g | Total Carbs: 54.2 g | Protein: 12.9 g.

Honey Dipped Waffles

Servings: 4 - 6 | Prep Time: 20 minutes | Cook Time: 10 minutes

Turn your morning sweet tooth into a waffle extravaganza with these yummy Honey Dipped Waffles. Best served with a cup of hot coffee, these waffles are also great with a side of your favorite lean protein and a cup of fruit.

Ingredients

1/2 cup gluten-free oat flour, or gluten-free all-purpose blend

1/2 cup sweet rice flour

3 tablespoons almond meal

2 tablespoons sucanat, or coconut sugar/pure cane sugar

1 teaspoon baking powder

1/2 teaspoon salt

2 large eggs

1/4 cup unsweetened almond milk

1/4 cup unsweetened applesauce

1/2 cup + 3 tablespoons honey, divided

2 tablespoons olive oil

1 teaspoon pure vanilla extract

Instructions

1. Preheat the waffle maker.

2. Add the oat flour, sweet rice flour, almond meal, sucanat, baking powder, and salt to a large mixing bowl and whisk until well combined.

3. In a separate mixing bowl, whisk the eggs.

4. Fold in the milk, applesauce, 3 tablespoons honey, olive oil, and pure vanilla extract.

5.   Pour the wet mixture into the dry ingredients and whisk together until just combined; do not over mix.

6.   Set the batter aside to rest for 10 minutes undisturbed.

7.   Pour one 1/2 cup batter into the waffle maker.

8.   Cook 3 - 4 minutes or until golden and fluffy.

9.   Transfer the waffles to a cooling rack and continue cooking waffles until all of the batter is used.

10.   Bring the honey to a low boil, in a medium saucepan over low-medium heat, whisking occasionally.

11.   Turn off the heat and pour in a shallow bowl just large enough to dip the waffles.

12.   Using caution, as the honey is very hot, dip the top of the waffle in the honey and let the excess drip off.

13.   Place on a cooling rack for 1 - 2 additional minutes and serve warm.

Nutritional Info: Calories: 306 | Sodium: 471 mg | Dietary Fiber: 1.7 g | Total Fat:8.7 g | Total Carbs: 55.2 g | Protein: 4.7 g.

Leftover Pizza Waffle

Servings: 1 | Prep Time: 0 minutes | Cook Time: 4 minutes

Some people will agree that there's nothing better for breakfast than left over pizza. For the pizza lover at heart, these Leftover Pizza Waffles are the perfect way to reheat leftover pizza and turn it into something truly spectacular.

Ingredients

2 slices leftover pizza

Instructions

1. Preheat the waffle maker.
2. Fold the point of the pizza slice up to one side of the crust.
3. Cut the crust off with scissors, at a diagonal, to make a triangle. Repeat with second slice.
4. Place both slices to fit as one big square into the waffle maker.
5. Cook 2 - 3 minutes or until golden brown. Serve with extra sauce for dipping!

Nutritional Info: Calories: 336 | Sodium: 680 mg | Dietary Fiber: 2.2 g | Total Fat:12.2 g | Total Carbs: 40.8 g | Protein: 15.2 g.

Lemon Blueberry Waffles

Servings: 2 - 4 | Prep Time: 5 minutes | Cook Time: 10 minutes

Give yourself a fresh outlook on breakfast with these zesty, sweet Lemon Blueberry Waffles! Simply sweet with a little citrus kick, these waffles are best served with a creamy topping for one lush waffle experience.

Ingredients

1 teaspoon lemon juice

1 tablespoon lemon zest

1/2 cup vegetable oil

1 cup 2% milk

2 eggs

1 cup sugar or 1/2 cup sugar substitute

1 3/4 cups flour

1 teaspoon baking powder

1 cup blueberries, fresh or frozen

Non-stick cooking spray

Crème fraiche

Instructions

1. Preheat the waffle maker.

2. In a large mixing bowl, whisk together the lemon juice, oil, milk, eggs, and sugar.

3. Add the flour and baking powder and whisk until well combined. Fold in the blueberries and lemon zest.

4. Fill the waffle iron with 3/4 cups of batter. Cook for 2 - 3 minutes or until golden and fluffy.

5. Transfer to a plate and carefully wipe off any blueberries that stuck to the iron before adding more batter for your next waffle; cook the remaining batter. Serve with a dollop of crème fraiche or whipped cream!

Nutritional Info: Calories: 713 | Sodium: 62 | Dietary Fiber: 2.5 g | Total Fat: 31.4 g | Total Carbs: 101.1 g | Protein: 10.8 g.

Power Waffles

Servings: 4 - 6 | Prep Time: 1 hour 10 minutes | Cook Time: 10 minutes

Start your day off right with Power Waffles. These waffles are exactly what you need to put some power into your step and really get your day going!

Ingredients

2 1/2 cups warm light soy milk, room temperature

1/4 cup minced crystallized ginger

2 tablespoons sugar

1 teaspoon dry yeast

1 1/2 cups unbleached all-purpose flour

1 cup buckwheat flour

1 cup old-fashioned oats

2 teaspoons ground cinnamon

1 teaspoon sea salt

6 large egg whites, beaten to blend

6 tablespoons unsalted butter, melted

2 teaspoons baking powder

1 cup plain low-fat yogurt

Non-stick cooking spray

6 ripe bananas, sliced for topping

Honey or pure maple syrup, for topping

3/4 cups sliced almonds, toasted for topping

Instructions

1. Mix first 4 ingredients in medium mixing bowl to blend. Let stand until foamy, about 10 minutes.

2. Mix both flours, oats, cinnamon and salt in large mixing bowl.

3. Add yeast mixture; stir to blend until batter is thick. Cover and chill at least 1 hour or overnight.

4.   Preheat Cuisinart Belgian Waffle Maker and preheat oven to 200° Fahrenheit.

5.   Mix the egg whites, melted butter and baking powder into batter.

6.   Spoon 1 cup batter onto waffle maker and spread evenly with a spatula.

7.   Grease both sides of the waffle maker.

8.   Cook 3 - 4 minutes or until golden and fluffy.

9.   Transfer waffle to baking sheet and keep warm in oven. Repeat, making 6 waffles total.

10.   Place waffles on plates. Top with yogurt, bananas, honey and almonds and enjoy.

Nutritional Info: Calories: 616 | Sodium: 514 mg | Dietary Fiber: 10.2 g | Total Fat:21.3 g | Total Carbs: 91.4 g | Protein: 20.5 g.

True Belgian Waffle

Servings: 4 – 6 | Prep Time: 10 minutes | Cook Time: 20 minutes

Make breakfast an occasion with fresh homemade waffles using your Cuisinart Belgian Waffle Maker. Whip up fluffy, golden waffles right in the comfort of your own kitchen and serve them up with fresh fruit, syrup or powdered sugar for one delicious experience.

Ingredients

2 cups all-purpose flour

3/4 cups sugar or sugar substitute

3 1/2 teaspoons baking powder

2 large eggs, separated

1 1/2 cups milk

1 cup unsalted butter, melted

1 teaspoon pure vanilla extract

Fresh strawberries, sliced for topping

Maple syrup, for topping

Powdered sugar, for topping

Instructions

1. Preheat the waffle maker.

2. Combine flour, sugar and baking powder in a mixing bowl.

3. In a second mixing bowl, lightly beat the egg yolks.

4. Fold the milk, butter and vanilla into the egg yolks and mix well.

5. Fold dry ingredients into the egg mixture until just combined.

6. Beat egg whites in a metal mixing bowl until stiff peaks form; fold into batter.

7. Pour approximately 3/4 to 1 cup of waffle batter into the center of the bottom waffle grid until covered, but not leaking over the side.

8. Cook 2-3 minutes or until waffle is golden and fluffy.

9. Dust waffles with powdered sugar. Top with strawberries or syrup and serve hot.

Nutritional Info: Calories: 691 | Sodium: 328 mg | Dietary Fiber: 1.4 g | Total Fat: 40.8 g | Total Carbs: 73.7 g | Protein: 10.5 g.

Vanilla Waffle

Servings: 2 | Prep Time: 5 minutes | Cook Time: 5 minutes

Whip up some creamy vanilla waffles and take your taste buds somewhere sweet for breakfast. This delicious waffle takes on the decadent mild flavor of vanilla for a waffle that is a little taste of heaven. Serve it classic style with butter and syrup or topped with nut butter for a little extra decadent protein boost.

Ingredients

7 tablespoons butter, softened

6 tablespoons pure maple syrup

4 eggs

1 teaspoon vanilla sugar

1/4 cup all-purpose flour

3 1/2 tablespoons corn flour

1 teaspoon baking powder

3 tablespoons ground almonds

4 tablespoons half and half

1 pinch salt

Instructions

1. Beat the butter until fluffy.

2. Add the maple syrup.

3. Separate the eggs.

4. Mix the egg yolks with the butter and vanilla until frothy.

5. Mix the flour, cornstarch and baking powder into the butter mixture.

6. Add the almonds and half and half; add this to the egg yolk mixture and beat with an electric mixer until smooth.

7. Beat the egg whites with the salt and fold into the batter.

8.   Spoon 3/4 cup batter into the waffle maker
9.   Cook the waffle for 2 - 3 minutes or until the steam has ceased.
10. Serve with your favorite toppings or on its own!

Nutritional Info: Calories: 842 | Sodium: 508 | Dietary Fiber: 2.5 g | Total Fat: 57.7 g |
Total Carbs: 69.1 g | Protein: 16.8 g.

Waffle Iron Omelets

Servings: 8 | Prep Time: 15 minutes | Cook Time: 20 minutes

Reinvent breakfast with clean eating at its finest! Waffle Iron Omelets are absolutely delicious, nutritious and healthy. These protein packed waffles will transform how you do breakfast in just a few easy steps.

Ingredients

3 whole eggs

1/4 cup grated parmesan

1/2 cup finely chopped onions

1/2 cup finely chopped green peppers

1/2 teaspoon garlic powder

1/4 teaspoon oregano

1/2 teaspoon olive oil

Fresh tomatoes, chopped for topping grated

Cheddar cheese, for topping

Instructions

1. Preheat the waffle maker.

2. Beat the eggs in a large mixing bowl.

3. Whisk in the parmesan, onions, peppers, garlic powder, oregano and olive oil until well combined.

4. Spray the Cuisinart Belgian Waffle Maker with non-stick cooking spray.

5. Pour just enough egg mixture onto the waffle iron to cover the entire surface area and try not to overfill.

6. Set the Cuisinart timer by pressing the minutes and seconds buttons to the desired time.

7. Cook 2 - 3 minutes or until done.

8. Top with some grated cheddar cheese and fresh chopped tomatoes and serve.

Nutritional Info: Calories: 54 | Sodium: 89 mg | Dietary Fiber: 0.0 g | Total Fat: 3.5 g | Total Carbs: 1.5 g | Protein: 4.5 g.

Waffled Banana Bread

Servings: 4 | Prep Time: 10 minutes | Cook Time: 15 minutes

Take this Southern brunch classic and turn it into yummy waffles in just a few easy steps. Serve this up with a side of your favorite lean breakfast protein or top it off with butter and maple syrup for step up to the classic banana bread treat.

Ingredients

1 1/4 cups all-purpose flour

3/4 cups granulated sugar

1/2 cup chopped walnuts

1 teaspoon baking powder

1/2 teaspoon baking soda

1/2 teaspoon ground cinnamon

1/2 teaspoon nutmeg

1/4 teaspoon sea salt

3 ripe bananas, mashed

1/2 cup vegetable oil, plus more for brushing waffle maker

1/2 cup greek yogurt

1 teaspoon pure vanilla extract

2 large eggs

Butter, for topping

Syrup, for topping

Instructions

1. Preheat the Cuisinart Belgian Waffle maker and an oven to 200 degrees Fahrenheit.

2. Whisk together the flour, sugar, walnuts, baking powder, baking soda, cinnamon, nutmeg and salt in a large mixing bowl.

3. Whisk together the banana, oil, Greek yogurt, vanilla and eggs in another mixing bowl.

4. Fold the banana mixture into the flour mixture until just combined.

5.   Lightly brush the top and bottom of the waffle iron with oil.

6.   Fill each section about three-quarters of the way full.

7.   Cook until the waffles are golden brown, 4 to 6 minutes.

8.   Keep the waffles warm in the oven while you cook the remaining batter.

9.   Spread with butter, drizzle with syrup and serve.

Nutritional Info: Calories: 763 | Sodium: 335 | Dietary Fiber: 4.7 g | Total Fat: 40.1 g | Total Carbs: 92.5 g | Protein: 13.7 g.

Waffled Biscuits

Servings: 4 | Prep Time: 10 minutes | Cook Time: 15 minutes

Waffle up a taste of the deep south with these scrumptious "stick to your ribs" Waffle Biscuits. Perfect with a bloody mary or sparkling spa water, these waffles will soon become a breakfast favorite.

Ingredients

2 teaspoons olive oil

8 ounces breakfast sausage, removed from casings

2 packages peppered or country gravy

8 rounds refrigerated biscuit dough, separated

Non-stick cooking spray

Instructions

1. Heat the oil in a large nonstick skillet over medium-high heat. Add the sausage and cook for 5 minutes, breaking it up with a wooden spoon, until browned and cooked through.

2. Preheat the waffle maker. with non-stick cooking spray.

3. Prepare gravy as directed on the package.

4. Fold sausage into gravy and keep warm on the stove.

5. Place 1 biscuit round into each section of your waffle iron.

6. Close lid gently, grasp both handles and flip the waffle maker over 180°.

7. Cook for 3 - 4 minutes, until golden. Repeat with the remaining four biscuits.

8. Place 2 biscuits per plate and top with the sausage gravy.

Nutritional Info: Calories: 370 | Sodium: 1436 mg | Dietary Fiber: 0.0 g | Total Fat:24.3 g | Total Carbs: 28.0 g | Protein: 15.2 g.

Whole Wheat Belgian Waffles

Servings: 5 | Prep Time: 10 minutes | Cook Time: 20 minutes

Start your day the healthy way with these delicious Whole Wheat Belgian Waffles. Diabetic and cholesterol healthy, these yummy waffles are made with whole wheat flour so you can still have waffles without the refined carbs.

Ingredients

2 cups whole flour

1/4 cup sugar or sugar substitute

3 tablespoons baking powder

3 eggs, separated

2 cups milk

1/3 cup vegetable oil

1 teaspoon pure vanilla extract

Instructions

1. Preheat the waffle maker.
2. Combine flour, sugar and baking powder in a mixing bowl.
3. In a second mixing bowl, lightly beat the egg yolks.
4. Fold the milk, oil and vanilla into the egg yolks and mix well.
5. Fold dry ingredients into the egg mixture until just combined.
6. Beat egg whites in a metal mixing bowl until stiff peaks form; fold into batter.
7. Pour approximately 3/4 to 1 cup of waffle batter into the center of the bottom waffle griddle.
8. Cook for 2 -3 minutes.
9. Top with syrup or your favorite waffle toppings to serve.

Nutritional Info: Calories: 557 | Sodium: 115 | Dietary Fiber: 1.9 g | Total Fat: 24.6 g | Total Carbs: 71.8 g | Protein: 14.6 g.

Yeast Waffles

Servings: 2 - 4 | Prep Time: 24 hours 15 minutes | Cook Time: 10 minutes

Yeast makes for one decadent base in this yummy waffle recipe. Whether you like your waffles classically topped with butter and syrup or decked out with crème fraiche and fruit—you're going to love these Yeast Waffles.

Ingredients

1 package active dry yeast

3 1/4 cups all-purpose flour

2 cups milk, warmed

2 eggs, slightly beaten

1/2 cup vegetable oil

Instructions

1. Mix eggs, salt, sugar and oil in a large bowl.

2. Heat milk to lukewarm.

3. Sift flour into bowl and add warm milk and yeast dissolved in water; mix well.

4. Cover the bowl tightly with plastic wrap and refrigerate overnight.

5. Pour one 1/2 cup batter into center of the waffle maker.

6. Cook for 2 - 4 minutes or until golden and fluffy; repeat until batter is gone.

7. Top with your favorite toppings and enjoy!

Nutritional Info: Calories: 708 | Sodium: 91 | Dietary Fiber: 3.1 g | Total Fat: 33.0 g | Total Carbs: 84.3 g | Protein: 17.9 g.

7

Lunch & Dinner Waffles

BLT Waffle

Servings: 2 | Prep Time: 5 minutes | Cook Time: 10 minutes

Turn lunchtime or dinner into a waffle extravaganza with the BLT Waffle. Perfect any day of the week, this quick and easy recipe will soon become a waffle maker favorite. Serve it up with a glass of iced tea and a cup of fruit for a full on healthy meal option.

Ingredients

2 cups all-purpose flour

3/4 cups sugar or sugar substitute

3 1/2 teaspoons baking powder

2 large eggs, separated

1 1/2 cups milk

1 cup unsalted butter, melted

1 teaspoon pure vanilla extract

12 slices bacon, prepared

4 slices beefsteak tomato

4 leaves iceberg lettuce, rinsed and dried with a paper towel

4 tablespoons sugar free mayonnaise, like Duke's

Instructions

1. Preheat the waffle maker.

2. Combine flour, sugar and baking powder in a mixing bowl.

3. In a second mixing bowl, lightly beat the egg yolks.

4. Fold the milk, butter and vanilla into the egg yolks and mix well.

5. Fold dry ingredients into the egg mixture until just combined.

6. Beat egg whites in a metal mixing bowl until stiff peaks form; fold into batter.

7. Pour approximately 3/4 to 1 cup of waffle batter into the center of the bottom waffle grid until covered, but not leaking over the side.

8. Cook for 3 minutes.

9. Assemble BLTs by spreading 1 tablespoon of mayonnaise on each waffle.

10. Top mayonnaise side up with 6 slices of bacon, 2-piece lettuce and 2 slices of tomato.

11. Place second waffle on top, mayonnaise side down, and serve.

Nutritional Info: Calories: 1385 | Sodium: 2480 | Dietary Fiber: 2.0 g | Total Fat: 91.5 g | Total Carbs: 97.5 g | Protein: 44.9 g.

Chana Masala Waffles

Servings: 4 | Prep Time: 5 minutes | Cook Time: 10 minutes

Mix the best of both worlds and spice things up for late lunch or dinner with these spicy Chana Masala Waffles. Warm and savory, these waffles will fill your senses with a taste of India.

Ingredients

2 flax eggs (2 tablespoons flax meal mixed with 6 tablespoons warm water)

1 cup chickpea flour

1/4 cup nutritional yeast

1 teaspoon baking powder

1 teaspoon coconut sugar, or other vegan sugar

1 teaspoon chana masala spice blend

1/2 teaspoon ground cumin

1/2 teaspoon smoked paprika

1/2 teaspoon ground cilantro

1/2 teaspoon turmeric

1/2 teaspoon black salt

1/8 teaspoon cayenne pepper

1/2 teaspoon baking soda

Black pepper to taste

1 clove garlic, chopped

1/4-inch ginger, peeled and chopped

1 tablespoon tomato paste

3/4 cups milk

1/4 cup canola oil

1 jar of mango chutney

Instructions

1. Prepare your flax eggs. Set aside.
2. Preheat the waffle maker.

3. Pulse the garlic, ginger, tomato paste and the milk, about 10 times, in a food processor or blender until mostly smooth.

4. Combine the dry ingredients in a large mixing bowl.

5. In a separate medium mixing bowl, combine the wet ingredients and the flax eggs.

6. Fold in the dry ingredients and stir to combine.

7. Scoop 3/4 cups batter into the waffle maker.

8. Cook until golden and fluffy, about 3 minutes. Transfer to a plate and tent with aluminum foil to keep warm; continue to cook waffles until all of the batter is used.

9. Top with mango chutney and serve!

Nutritional Info: Calories: 479 | Sodium: 613 | Dietary Fiber: 12.7 g | Total Fat: 19.5 g | Total Carbs: 65.5 g | Protein: 16.9 g.

Chicken, Broccoli, Cheddar & Potato Waffles

Servings: 4-6 | Prep Time: 40 minutes | Cook Time: 10 minutes

Transform traditional dinner into fabulous with these delicious little waffles. Packed full of protein, vegetables and gooey cheese - these melt in your mouth waffles are the perfect comfort food on a cold day or family fun night in.

Ingredients

5 yukon gold potatoes, peeled

1/3 cup 2% milk

3 tablespoons butter, unsalted

1 1/3 cups rotisserie chicken, chopped

1 cup cheddar cheese, shredded

1 1/3 cups broccoli, boiled and finely chopped

1/2 teaspoon sea salt

1/4 teaspoon coarse ground black pepper

1 cup all-purpose flour

1 large egg

Instructions

1. Preheat the waffle maker.
2. Bring a saucepan filled with water to a boil on high heat. Add the potatoes and boil 30 minutes or until tender.
3. Drain and transfer potatoes to a large mixing bowl.
4. Mash the potatoes; add milk and butter. Mix until well-incorporated.
5. Fold in the salt, pepper, flour and egg and mix until well-blended.
6. Fold in the chicken, cheese and broccoli.
7. Pour in 1/3 cup batter.

8.   Cook until slightly brown and serve hot!

Nutritional Info: Calories: 406 | Sodium: 530 | Dietary Fiber: 5.4 g | Total Fat: 13.9 g | Total Carbs: 47.2 g | Protein: 24.1 g.

Cornbread Waffles

Servings: 4 | Prep Time: 10 minutes | Cook Time: 10 minutes

Waffles aren't just for breakfast. These savory, sweet and very tasty Cornbread Waffles are the perfect treat for lunch or dinner. Topped with Chipotle Syrup and stuffed with some sweet Southern greens - these waffles are simply divine.

Ingredients

1 1/4 cups spelt flour

1 1/4 cups cornmeal

1/4 cup flaxseed (ground)

1/2 cup aged cheddar, shredded

1/2 teaspoon ground chipotle pepper

2 cups milk or almond milk

2 tablespoons apple cider vinegar

3 tablespoons coconut oil (melted)

2 large eggs

1 teaspoon sea salt

1 cup collard greens, de-ribbed and chopped

For the Chipotle Syrup:

1/2 chipotle pepper, in adobo sauce

1/4 cup maple syrup

Instructions

1. Preheat the waffle maker.

2. Whisk milk and apple cider vinegar together in a large mixing bowl. Add eggs and coconut oil; mix until well-blended.

3. Add flour, corn meal, ground flax seed, chipotle powder, and sea salt to the milk mixture and stir well.

4. Fold in cheddar until well incorporated.

5. Spray waffle maker with non-stick cooking spray.

6. Scoop 1/2 cup batter into the waffle maker.

7. Add a handful of greens on top, and top with another 1/2 cup of batter.

8. Chop the chipotle as finely as possible, and stir into the syrup until well-blended. Top each waffle with syrup and serve.

Nutritional Info: Calories: 756 | Sodium: 714 | Dietary Fiber: 12.3 g | Total Fat: 47.6 g | Total Carbs: 66.6 g | Protein: 22.6 g.

Crab Cake Waffles

Servings: 3 | Prep Time: 10 minutes | Cook Time: 10 minutes

Spice things up for dinner and whip up some delicious Crab Cake Waffles for the whole family. These delicious little waffles, inspired by the classic crab cake, are best served with a side salad and a glass of sweet iced tea.

Ingredients

10 ounces crabmeat, drained and rinsed

1 tablespoon coconut flour

2 tablespoons almond flour

1/4 cup red bell pepper, finely diced

1/4 teaspoon dry mustard

1/2 teaspoon minced onion

1/2 teaspoon garlic powder

1/8 teaspoon sea salt

1/8 teaspoon black pepper

1/2 teaspoon dried parsley

Dash of cayenne pepper

1 teaspoon lemon juice

1 teaspoon sugar-free mayonnaise

1 free range egg

Non-stick cooking spray

Instructions

1. Preheat the waffle maker.

2. Combine egg, lemon juice and mayonnaise in a large metal mixing bowl using a whisk.

3. Whisk in all of the spices and flour.

4. Fold in the red pepper and crab meat.

5. Spread a handful of the crab cake evenly across the waffle maker.

6. Cook for 3 minutes.

7. Serve while hot with your favorite salad!

Nutritional Info: Calories: 141 | Sodium: 906 | Dietary Fiber: 1.2 g | Total Fat: 3.8 g | Total Carbs: 16.5 g | Protein: 9.8 g.

Deep Dish Pizza

Servings: 4 | Prep Time: 6 hours 10 minutes | Cook Time: 10 minutes

Bring a taste of Chicago right into your own kitchen with these scrumptious little Deep Dish Pizza waffles. Serve them up with a side salad and a glass of wine and you've got one seriously decadent meal.

Ingredients

2 1/4 teaspoons active dry yeast

1 1/2 teaspoons granulated sugar

1 1/8 cups warm water

3 cups all-purpose flour

1/2 cup olive oil

1 1/2 teaspoons sea salt

4 tablespoons butter, melted (to brush on top of each waffle)

Grated parmesan, for dusting

Garlic salt, for dusting

For the Filling:

1 (14-ounce) can fire roasted tomatoes

1 teaspoon garlic powder

1 teaspoon dried oregano

8 slices fresh mozzarella cheese

1 cup mozzarella cheese, shredded

20 slices pepperoni

Instructions

1.   Put the yeast, sugar, and water in a large bowl and let it stand for five minutes until it starts looking foamy. After the yeast foams, stir in the flour one cup at a time.

2.   Add the oil and salt once the dough starts to form into a sticky ball.

3. Knead for 3 - 4 minutes with your hands; the dough will be tacky and form into a ball easily. If the dough is still too sticky, add an additional 1/4 cup of flour and knead for 3 - 4 more minutes.

4. Place the dough into a large mixing bowl. Cover with a clean towel and place in a warm corner of the kitchen to rise, about 6 hours, until double in size.

5. Divide into four small dough balls.

6. Divide one of the four balls in half. User your palm to flatten the half piece of dough into a circle (about six inches wide).

7. Top with a few tablespoons of sauce. Smooth the sauce into a circle, leaving one 1/2-inch border around the circle edges.

8. Top the sauce with two slices fresh mozzarella, 1/4 cup shredded mozzarella, and five pieces of pepperoni.

9. Flatten the other half of the dough into an equal sized circle and put it on top of the toppings.

10. Seal the edges with your fingers so that the two pieces form one ball of stuffed dough.

11. Brush the top with melted butter and dust with a Parmesan and garlic powder. Repeat with the remaining dough balls.

12. Spray both sides of the waffle iron griddle with nonstick cooking spray.

13. Place a deep dish waffle on the waffle maker.

14. Cook until lightly browned and crispy, about 3 minutes. Repeat for the remaining deep dish waffles and enjoy.

Nutritional Info: Calories: 671 | Sodium: 789 | Dietary Fiber: 3.0 g | Total Fat: 37.7 g | Total Carbs: 73.9 g | Protein: 10.7 g.

Frittaffle

Servings: 4 | Prep Time: 2 hours 20 minutes | Cook Time: 10 minutes

When the frittata meets the waffle, you've got one seriously amazing meal. Stuffed with scrumptious ingredients and tantalizing treats - you'll quickly fall in love with this amazing recipe. Serve it up with a side salad and a glass of wine or sparkling water for one sophisticated waffle meal.

Ingredients

1 tablespoon olive oil

1 large red bell pepper, diced

2 cups roasted potatoes, cubed

2 cups arugula, chopped

8 pieces bacon, broken into 1-inch pieces

Sea salt and pepper to taste

8 large eggs, whisked and combined

1/2 cup parmesan cheese, shaved

1 cup mozzarella cheese, shredded

Instructions

1. Preheat an oven to 375 degrees Fahrenheit.

2. Add olive oil to a nonstick, ovenproof skillet and heat on medium heat. Stir in red peppers and cook until soft.

3. Add in potatoes and stir until warmed through. Fold in arugula and bacon and stir to combine with the other ingredients.

4. Combine salt, pepper, parmesan cheese and eggs in a mixing bowl.

5. Pour egg mixture evenly across the pan of pepper and potato mixture; distribute it throughout.

6. Stir in 3/4 cups of mozzarella and sprinkle the remaining 1/4 cup on top.

7. Cook over medium high heat for another 1-2 minutes or just until a slightly crust forms around the edge.

8. Transfer pan to oven and bake for about 8 to 10 minutes or until set.

9. Remove pan from the oven and slide the frittata out to cool on a wire rack for 5 to 10 minutes.

10. Transfer to refrigerator and let chill for at least two hours.

11. Remove from refrigerator and use a round 2.5-inch ring to stamp out rounds.

12. Preheat the waffle maker. Place a round in the center and heat until warmed through and waffled golden crisp.

Nutritional Info: Calories: 798 | Sodium: 2062 | Dietary Fiber: 19.2 g | Total Fat: 53.5 g | Total Carbs: 19.2 g | Protein: 60.6 g.

Ham & Gruyere Belgian Waffle

Servings: 4 - 6 | Prep Time: 10 minutes | Cook Time: 20 minutes

When Belgium meets a taste of France you get one truly European inspired waffle. Perfect for lunch or dinner, this waffle is also great for a brunch time menu too. Just don't forget the champagne!

Ingredients

2 cups all-purpose flour

3/4 cups sugar or sugar substitute

3 1/2 teaspoons baking powder

2 large eggs, separated

1 1/2 cups milk

1 cup unsalted butter, melted

1 teaspoon pure vanilla extract

For Topping:

4 slices gruyere cheese

8 slices ham

3 tablespoons grainy Dijon mustard

1 whole pear, super-thin sliced

Instructions

1. Preheat an oven to 200 degrees Fahrenheit.
2. Combine flour, sugar and baking powder in a mixing bowl.
3. In a second mixing bowl, lightly beat the egg yolks.
4. Fold the milk, butter and vanilla into the egg yolks and mix well.
5. Fold dry ingredients into the egg mixture until just combined.

6.   Beat egg whites in a metal mixing bowl until stiff peaks form; fold into batter.

7.   Pour approximately 3/4 to 1 cup of waffle batter into the center of the bottom waffle grid until covered.

8.   Cook for 2 - 3 minutes. Remove and top each waffle with cheese and transfer to a warm oven to melt.

9.   Remove waffles from oven once all batter has been used. Top with ham and a slice or two of pear and serve!

Nutritional Info: Calories: 753 | Sodium: 824| Dietary Fiber: 3.2 g | Total Fat: 44.9 g |
Total Carbs: 68.4 g | Protein: 22.0 g.

Peanut Butter French Toast Waffle

Servings: 2 | Prep Time: 5 minutes | Cook Time: 5 minutes

Pack your waffle with peanut butter for some healthy protein! This twist on the classic lunchtime favorite peanut butter sandwich is absolutely out of this world. Best served with a cold glass of your favorite kind of milk, you'll fall in love with this waffle recipe.

Ingredients

1 cup half and half

1 large egg

4 slices thick white bread

4 tablespoons peanut butter

Sliced bananas, for topping

Instructions

1. Whisk together the half and half and eggs in a shallow mixing bowl until well-blended.

2. Submerge one slice of bread in the egg mixture until well-coated. Let it soak in, then move the bread to the waffle iron.

3. Spoon 2 tablespoons of peanut butter into the center of the bread. Lay a second piece of bread on top.

4. Cook for 3 minutes or until golden brown: repeat until all bread is cooked.

5. Top with sliced.

Nutritional Info: Calories: 429 | Sodium: 354 | Dietary Fiber: 2.3 g | Total Fat: 33.1 g | Total Carbs: 20.8 g | Protein: 16.1 g.

Pepperoni Stuffed Waffle Biscuits

Servings: 1 serving | Prep Time: 5 minutes | Cook Time: 5 minutes

Get your waffle on with these quick and easy Pepperoni Stuffed Waffle Biscuits. Turn your Cuisinart Belgian Waffle Maker into a pepperoni roll press and serve these up for a quick lunch or dinner when you're on the go.

Ingredients

1 can refrigerated biscuits, like Pillsbury

1 cups mozzarella cheese, shredded

10 slices of pepperoni

Non-stick cooking spray

Pizza sauce for dipping, optional

Instructions

1. Lay biscuits out on a work surface.

2. Top two with mozzarella cheese, 5 pepperoni slices each, and another layer of mozzarella cheese.

3. Finish topping with a second biscuit and lightly sandwich together.

4. Place one biscuit on each side of the waffle maker griddle.

5. Cook for 3-4 minutes or until golden and crispy.

6. Serve piping hot with pizza sauce for dipping!

Nutritional Info: Calories: 912 | Sodium: 2269 | Dietary Fiber: 0.0 g | Total Fat: 64.2 g | Total Carbs: 8.0 g | Protein: 76.5 g.

Potato Waffle

Servings: 2 | Prep Time: 5 minutes | Cook Time: 10 minutes

Sometimes a little leftover comfort food can go a long way. Use your Cuisinart Belgian Waffle Maker to transform those delicious leftover potatoes into something absolutely brilliant. Topped with chicken and gravy for a taste of the south or just on its own—these waffles don't disappoint.

Ingredients

2 tablespoons unsalted butter

1/4 cup buttermilk, melted

2 eggs

2 cups leftover mashed potatoes

3 tablespoons garlic, minced

1/4 cup all-purpose flour

1/8 teaspoon sea salt

1/8 teaspoon fresh ground black pepper

Instructions

1. Grease and preheat the Cuisinart Belgian Waffle Maker.

2. Melt butter in a small saucepan over medium-low heat and set aside to cool.

3. Add the leftover mashed potatoes, garlic, salt and pepper and gently stir to combine.

4. Whisk in eggs until thoroughly combined.

5. Fold in the flour until just combined; do not to overmix the batter.

6. Spoon 1/4 cup batter into the waffle maker.

7. Cook the waffle for 2 - 3 minutes or until the steam has ceased.

8. Serve with chicken and gravy or with sour cream as a dipping sauce!

Nutritional Info: Calories: 454 | Sodium: 845 | Dietary Fiber: 0.7 g | Total Fat: 19.3 g | Total Carbs: 57.1 g | Protein: 14.7 g.

Puffles

Servings: 6 - 8 | Prep Time: 15 minutes | Cook Time: 10 minutes

Take puff pastry and waffles and what do you get? Puffles! No matter what you like to stuff in the Puffles—you'll fall in love with these quick and easy treats.

Ingredients

Flour, for dusting work surface

1 (17-ounce) box of puff pastry, thawed

Water, for brushing

For S'mores Puffles:

2/3 cups chocolate chips

1 cup mini marshmallows

Lightly sweetened whipped cream, for serving

For Croque Monsieur Puffles:

1/2-pound Gruyere or Swiss cheese, grated (about 1 1/3 cups)

8 slices ham (about 6 ounces)

3 tablespoons grainy Dijon mustard

Non-stick cooking spray, butter flavored

Instructions

1. Lightly flour a work surface.

2. Unroll the pastry and cut it in half width-wise.

3. Measure the cooking surface of your waffle maker. Roll each piece of pastry to the same width but double the length of your

94

waffle maker. For example, if your waffle maker measures 8 inches square, roll each piece of pastry to an 8x16-inch rectangle.

4. Divide the filling ingredients of your choice between the two pieces of pastry evenly, on one half of each piece of dough, leaving a 1/2-inch border.

5. Lightly brush border with water.

6. Fold the other half of each piece of pastry over like a book and trim the edges to fit in a circle, then crimp the edges to seal the filling in.

7. Place one filled waffle inside the waffle maker. Cook 5 to 6 minutes for each puffle until golden and fluffy.

8. Cut each puffle into four pieces and serve warm!

Nutritional Info: Calories: 644 | Sodium: 582 | Dietary Fiber: 1.9 g | Total Fat: 37.1 g | Total Carbs: 60.5 g | Protein: 17.1 g.

Turkey Melt Waffles

Servings: 1 | Prep Time: 5 minutes | Cook Time: 5 minutes

Put a seriously tantalizing spin on the traditional turkey melt with this delicious recipe! Turkey melts are great served alongside a hot bowl of soup or fresh garden salad.

Ingredients

Non-stick cooking spray

2 slices sourdough bread

2 slices monterey jack cheese

1 tablespoon olive oil, for brushing

Pinch of sea salt

Pinch of black pepper

1 teaspoon dijon mustard

1 tablespoon sugar-free mayonnaise

4 slices turkey

2 super-thin slices of tart apple

Instructions

1. Brush one side of each piece of bread with olive oil, and lay the slices on a plate oil side down.

2. Spread a thin layer of mustard and mayonnaise on each slice of the bread. Season each side of the bread with a pinch of salt and pepper.

3. Layer one slice of bread with a slice of cheese, top cheese with turkey, the two apple slices and the last piece of cheese.

4. Sandwich the pieces together and lay it onto the Cuisinart Belgian Waffle Maker.

5. Grill for 4 - 5 minutes or until the edges are browned and crispy and the cheese is melted. Serve warm with your favorite side!

Nutritional Info: Calories: 993 | Sodium: 1253| Dietary Fiber: 5.4 g | Total Fat: 47.5 g | Total Carbs: 61.1 g | Protein: 80.6 g.

Waffle Panini

Servings: 1 | Prep Time: 5 minutes | Cook Time: 5 minutes

Waffle Paninis are a great addition to any lunch on the go or quick and easy dinner at home. While this is my favorite way to stuff a panini, feel free to use your favorite stuffings too.

Ingredients

Non-stick cooking spray

2 slices sourdough bread

2 slices provolone cheese

1 tablespoon olive oil, for brushing

Pinch of sea salt

Pinch of black pepper

Handful of baby spinach

3 slices honey ham

2 thin slices of roma tomato

Instructions

1. Brush one side of each piece of bread with olive oil, and lay the slices on a plate oil side up.

2. Season each side of the bread with a pinch of salt and pepper. Layer one slice of bread with a slice of cheese, the baby spinach, honey ham, tomato and the last piece of cheese.

3. Sandwich the pieces together and lay it onto the Cuisinart Belgian Waffle Maker.

4. Grill for 4 minutes or until the edges are browned and crispy and the cheese is melted.

5. Serve warm!

Nutritional Info: Calories: 569 | Sodium: 1342 | Dietary Fiber: 5.0 g | Total Fat: 31.2 g | Total Carbs: 48.3 g | Protein: 27.3 g.

Waffle Sandwich

Servings: 1 | Prep Time: 5 minutes | Cook Time: 5 minutes

Turn your Cuisinart Belgian Waffle Maker into a sandwich maker with this delicious recipe. I love this twist on the classic Reuben sandwich, but you can stuff your waffle sandwich with anything your sandwich loving heart desires.

Ingredients

Non-stick cooking spray

Butter, for brushing

2 slices rye bread

2 tablespoons russian dressing

4 slices corned beef

2 thin slices of swiss cheese

Instructions

1. Brush one side of each piece of bread with butter, and lay the slices on a plate butter side down.

2. Layer one slice of bread with Russian dressing, a slice of cheese, corned beef, and the last piece of cheese.

3. Spread the remaining Russian dressing on the other slice of bread and sandwich it all together.

4. Lay the sandwich onto the Cuisinart Belgian Waffle Maker.

5. Cook for 4 -5 minutes or until the edges are browned and crispy and the cheese is melted.

6. Serve warm!

Nutritional Info: Calories: 161 | Sodium: 448| Dietary Fiber: 0.5 g | Total Fat: 10.1 g | Total Carbs: 6.7 g | Protein: 10.5 g.

Waffled Chorizo Cheese Quesadilla

Servings: 2 - 4 | Prep Time: 15 minutes | Cook Time: 15 minutes

Warm up with a savory waffled quesadilla for lunch or dinner. Full of spice and gooey cheese, this "stick to your ribs" waffled quesadilla is perfect on its own or with a side salad. Try dipping it in chipotle salsa for a little more bite to your day.

Ingredients

1 lime, juiced

1/4 small red onion, diced small

1/8 teaspoon sea salt

2 ounces cured chorizo, sliced and diced

Olive oil, for brushing tortillas

Four tortillas, cut to fit waffle maker

1 bag cheddar cheese, shredded

Sour cream, for garnish

Salsa, for garnish

Chopped avocado, for topping

Instructions

1. Combine the lime juice, onions and salt in a small glass mixing bowl and toss. Let sit for 15 minutes, at room temperature, until the onions are pink.

2. Add the chorizo to a medium nonstick skillet and heat over medium-high heat for about 5 minutes.

3. Add the onions and cook until soft, about 3 minutes.

4. Preheat the waffle maker.

5. Brush one side of 2 tortillas with oil and lay dry-side up on a work surface.

6. Cover both tortillas with 1/3 cup cheese. Add 1/3 cup chorizo mixture to both.

7.   Sandwich each with the remaining tortillas and brush the tops with oil.

8.   Cook until golden brown and the cheese is melted, 4 to 6 minutes. Repeat with the remaining quesadilla.

9.   Cut the quesadillas into wedges and top with avocado. Garnish with salsa and sour cream to serve.

Nutritional Info: Calories: 267 | Sodium: 465 | Dietary Fiber: 2.2 g | Total Fat: 17.9 g | Total Carbs: 13.9 g | Protein: 13.8 g.

Waffled Eggplant Parmesan

Servings: 4-6 | Prep Time: 40 minutes | Cook Time: 10 minutes

Whip up a taste of Italy right in your Cuisinart Belgian Waffle Maker. This earthy, delightful recipe is the perfect way to serve up something different for dinner. Add a little signature spaghetti sauce or pesto, and a glass of wine - and you'll feel like you're right on the Sicilian countryside.

Ingredients

1 medium eggplant, peeled and sliced

2 cups parmesan cheese, finely grated

1 large egg

1/2 cup milk

Non-stick cooking spray

Instructions

1. Add the egg and milk to a large mixing bowl and whisk to create an egg wash.

2. Fill a second bowl with the parmesan cheese.

3. Dip each a slice of eggplant into the egg wash then transfer to the parmesan cheese and coat well. Set aside on a plate and repeat until all eggplant slices are coated.

4. Add two or three pieces of parmesan or however many fit inside the waffle maker. Grill for 2-4 minutes or until golden brown.

5. Cook all pieces and serve with your favorite pasta and sauce or a side salad.

Nutritional Info: Calories: 284 | Sodium: 725 | Dietary Fiber: 2.7 g | Total Fat: 17.6 g | Total Carbs: 8.3 g | Protein: 26.8 g.

Waffled Falafel

Servings: 4 | Prep Time: 30 minutes | Cook Time: 20 minutes

Skip the deep fry and waffle your falafel for a super-savory healthy meal option. Packed with spices and topped with fresh veggies, this bad boy makes for one Mediterranean slice of waffled heaven.

Ingredients

1 teaspoon ground cumin

1 teaspoon kosher salt

1/2 teaspoon ground coriander

1/4 teaspoon cayenne pepper

2 large egg whites

2 cloves garlic, halved

1 (15-ounce) can chickpeas, rinsed

Chopped lettuce, for topping

Sliced tomato, for topping

Cucumbers, for topping

Sliced onions, for topping

Banana peppers, for topping

Fresh buffalo mozzarella, sliced

Olive oil for brushing and drizzle

Balsamic vinegar, for drizzling

Instructions

1. Preheat the waffle maker.
2. Combine the oil, cilantro, flour, parsley, baking powder, cumin, salt, coriander, cayenne, egg whites, garlic and chickpeas in a food processor or blender and pulse until smooth.
3. Lightly brush the top and bottom of the waffle maker with olive oil.
4. Fill the waffle iron about three-quarters of the way full with batter, about 3/4 cups.

5. Close the waffle iron lid, grasp both handles and flip the waffle maker over 180°. Cook until the falafel is golden brown and firm in the center, about 6 to 10 minutes.

6. Add your choice of toppings above. Drizzle with olive oil and balsamic vinegar—and serve!

7. Alternatively, you can serve this up inside warm pita bread and make it a hearty meal!

Nutritional Info: Calories: 400 | Sodium: 625 | Dietary Fiber: 18.6 g | Total Fat: 6.6 g | Total Carbs: 65.4 g | Protein: 22.5 g.

Waffled Filet

Servings: 1 | Prep Time: 5 minutes | Cook Time: 10 - 15 minutes

Take your Cuisinart Belgian Waffle Maker to a whole new level with the Waffled Filet. Who knew you could waffle steak? Get super-fancy and serve up one decadent, lush dinner when you quickly waffle the filet in lieu of grilling it!

Ingredients

2 teaspoons coarse sea salt

2 teaspoons fresh ground black pepper

8 ounces filet mignon steak

Nonstick cooking spray

Instructions

1. Preheat the waffle iron on high.
2. Coat both sides of the steak with the salt and pepper.
3. Coat both sides of the waffle iron grid with nonstick cooking spray.
4. Put the steak on the waffle iron as far away from the hinge as possible.
5. Close the Cuisinart Belgian Waffle Maker lid and cook for 8 minutes; check the temperature of the steak after 8 minutes if not cooked to your favorite temperature continue cooking for 2 minute intervals until done.
6. Remove the steak and place it on a cutting board.
7. Allow the steak to rest for several minutes then slice and serve with your favorite sides.

Nutritional Info: Calories: 417 | Sodium: 3976| Dietary Fiber: 1.1 g | Total Fat: 15.1 g | Total Carbs: 2.7 g | Protein: 64.1 g.

Waffled Pizza Pockets

Servings: 2 | Prep Time: 10 minutes | Cook Time: 15 minutes

Whip up your own homemade pizza pockets for one delicious, fresh lunch right in the comfort of your own kitchen. Try Waffled Pizza Pockets with a side of grilled vegetables to make one healthy meal!

Ingredients

1 (15-ounce) can pizza sauce

1 package pepperoni

1 cup mozzarella cheese, shredded

8 rounds refrigerated biscuit dough, separated

Non-stick cooking spray

Instructions

1. Lay biscuit rounds out onto a wax paper lined workspace.
2. Spoon 1 teaspoon of pizza sauce onto four biscuits. Top with a few slices of pepperoni and a pile of mozzarella cheese.
3. Top each biscuit with remaining biscuit rounds.
4. Place 1 pizza pocket into each section of your waffle iron.
5. Cook for 3 - 4 minutes, until golden brown.
6. Serve with pizza sauce for dipping!

Nutritional Info: Calories: 1033 | Sodium: 2537 | Dietary Fiber: 4.3 g | Total Fat: 63.9 g | Total Carbs: 75.7 g | Protein: 38.0 g.

Waffled Spaghetti Pie

Servings: 4 | Prep Time: 15 minutes | Cook Time: 15 minutes

Spaghetti pie might be the most delicious way to serve up your favorite al dente pasta thanks to the Cuisinart Belgian Waffle Maker. Serve your pie up with a side salad and garlic bread for one full on Italian style meal.

Ingredients

1/2 pound spaghetti

1/2 cup milk

2 large eggs, lightly beaten

1 teaspoon freshly ground black pepper

1 teaspoon sea salt, plus extra for boiling water

1 tablespoon olive oil

4 ounces pecorino romano cheese, finely grated

4 ounces provolone cheese, shredded

Tomato sauce, for serving

Instructions

1. Bring a large pot of salted water to a boil.

2. Add the spaghetti to the boiling water. Pour in olive oil. Cook, about 7 minutes, very al dente. **If you bite into a strand of pasta it should have a core of uncooked pasta in the cross section.

3. Drain the pasta and let it cool slightly.

4. In a large mixing bowl, whisk together the eggs, milk, salt and pepper.

5. Fold in the cheese.

6. Add the spaghetti and toss it to combine well and coat the pasta.

7. Preheat the waffle maker.

8. Overstuff the spaghetti into the waffle maker with 1/4 of the spaghetti.

9. Cook 5 minutes or until it starts to crisp.

10. Remove the spaghetti from the waffle iron and set aside on a plate.

11. Repeat Steps 5 through 8 with three more piles of spaghetti.

12. Serve with tomato sauce and enjoy!

Nutritional Info: Calories: 455 | Sodium: 1121 | Dietary Fiber: 0 g | Total Fat: 23.1 g | Total Carbs: 34.7 g | Protein: 26.9 g.

Waffled Tuna Melts

Servings: 1 | Prep Time: 5 minutes | Cook Time: 5 minutes

A twist on the classic tuna melt, this waffled sandwich is quick, easy and so delightful. While I love my tuna melt with a nice big bowl of tomato soup on the side, you can also serve the Waffled Tuna Melt with a handful of kettle chips to make it a meal!

Ingredients

Non-stick cooking spray

2 slices thick sliced whole wheat bread

1/2 cup cheddar cheese, shredded

2 tablespoons butter, for brushing

Pinch of black pepper

1 tablespoon sugar-free mayonnaise

1 (6-ounce) can chunk light tuna, drained

1 celery rib, finely chopped

Instructions

1. Combine cheese, tuna, mayonnaise, celery and pepper in a mixing bowl.
2. Brush one side of each piece of bread with butter, and lay the slices on a plate butter side down.
3. Spread a heaping layer of tuna mixture onto one piece of bread.
4. Sandwich the pieces together and lay it onto the Cuisinart.
5. Cook for 4 - 5 minutes or until the edges are browned and crispy and the cheese is melted.
6. Serve warm with your favorite side!

Nutritional Info: Calories: 780 | Sodium: 1403| Dietary Fiber: 3.9 g | Total Fat: 50.1 g | Total Carbs: 27.6 g | Protein: 55.2 g.

8

Snack Waffles

Buttered Waffles

Servings: 4 - 6 | Prep Time: 10 minutes | Cook Time: 5 minutes

Get downright simple when it comes to snacking. The only fluff in this tantalizing snack is the waffle itself! All you have to do is top it with your favorite butter and snack away.

Ingredients

3 eggs

1 1/2 cups milk

1 teaspoon baking soda

1 3/4 cups flour

2 tablespoons baking powder

1/2 teaspoon salt

1/2 cup vegetable oil

Ingredients

1. Preheat the waffle maker.

2. Mix the flour, baking soda, baking powder and salt in a large mixing bowl.

3. Mix the eggs, milk and oil in a separate mixing bowl.

4. Fold in the dry ingredients and mix until well-blended.

5. Pour enough mix into waffle iron to cover the entire griddle

6. Close the waffle maker lid. Set the timer for 3 minutes. Flip the waffle maker over.

7. Cook until golden and fluffy. Transfer to a plate and tent with aluminum foil to keep warm.

8. Continue to cook batter until all waffles are cooked.

9. Top each waffle with butter and serve warm!

Nutritional Info: Calories: 360 | Sodium: 469| Dietary Fiber: 1.1 g | Total Fat: 22.0 g | Total Carbs: 33.3 g | Protein: 8.5 g.

Cheesy Waffles

Servings: 4 | Prep Time: 5 minutes | Cook Time: 10 minutes

Give your tastebuds something sincerely savory in the afternoon as a little energizing pick me up. Cheesy waffles are super easy and quick for those afternoons when you just need something to tide you over until dinner.

Ingredients

2 cups all-purpose flour

1 1/2 teaspoons baking powder

1 teaspoon sea salt

1 teaspoon fresh ground black pepper

2 1/4cups buttermilk

4 tablespoons unsalted butter, melted

2 eggs

2 cups cheddar cheese, shredded

Instructions

1. Whisk the flour with the baking powder, salt and pepper in a large mixing bowl to combine.
2. In a separate mixing bowl, whisk the buttermilk with the butter and eggs to combine.
3. Add buttermilk mixture to the flour mixture and whisk well to combine.
4. Gently fold in the cheese.
5. Preheat an oven to 200° Fahrenheit.
6. Lightly spray the waffle maker with non-stick cooking spray.
7. Ladle 1/2 cup of batter into the waffle maker.
8. Cook for about 2 -3 minutes or until the cheese is melted and bubbling out or the waffle is golden browned.

9.   Keep the waffles warm, on a baking sheet, in the preheated oven while you cook the rest of the batter. Serve immediately or freeze for later.

**Note - To freeze: wrap the finished waffles tightly in plastic wrap, then seal them inside a zip locked plastic bag. Store in the freezer for up to three months. Reheat in a toaster or in a 300° Fahrenheit oven until crispy and warm.

Nutritional Info: Calories: 647 | Sodium: 1079| Dietary Fiber: 1.9 g | Total Fat: 34.3 g | Total Carbs: 56.4 g | Protein: 28.0 g.

Choco Oatmeal Waffles

Servings: 4 - 6 | Prep Time: 5 minutes | Cook Time: 10 minutes

The perfect complement to any glass of milk, these delicious waffles are perfect for snacking. You'll get the sweet sensation of decadent chocolate in every bite. Quick and easy to make, you can store these waffles in an airtight container for up to three days or in the refrigerator for one week.

Ingredients

1 stick unsalted butter, melted

1/2 cup plus 2 tablespoons light brown sugar, firmly packed

2 large eggs

1 teaspoon pure vanilla extract

3/4 cups unbleached all-purpose flour

1/2 teaspoon baking soda

1/4 teaspoon sea salt

1 1/2 cups old-fashioned rolled oats

1 cup semisweet chocolate chips

Nonstick cooking spray

Instructions

1. Add melted butter and sugar to a large mixing bowl; stir together until smooth.

2. Add eggs and vanilla and stir again until well-blended.

3. Whisk in the flour, soda and salt.

4. Add chocolate chips and rolled oats until well-incorporated.

5. Scoop one teaspoon into each of the four griddles.

6. Close the waffle maker lid. Set the timer for 2 minutes. Flip the waffle maker over.

7. Lift the lid to check on the waffles; bake them for another 30 seconds if you want them more brown and crunchy.

8. Remove and set cool on a wire rack. Serve warm with your favorite kind of milk!

Nutritional Info: Calories: 746 | Sodium: 323| Dietary Fiber: 10.0 g | Total Fat: 32.6 g | Total Carbs: 101.7 g | Protein: 13.7 g.

Churros

Servings: 4 | Prep Time: 5 minutes | Cook Time: 10 minutes

Add a little Latin spice to your waffle life with deliciously sweet churros! Your Cuisinart Belgian Waffle Maker is the most easy, convenient way to get warm, spiced desserts right in the comfort of your own home. Serve them up with a pot of Mexican chocolate dipping sauce for one seriously decadent afternoon snack.

Ingredients

1 package (2 sheets) frozen puff pastry, thawed

Flour, for dusting

1/2 cup sugar

1 1/2 teaspoons cinnamon, divided

For Chocolate Dipping Sauce:

1 cup heavy cream

1 cup dark chocolate chips

1/2 teaspoon ancho chili powder

A pinch of salt

Instructions

1. Dust your work surface with a little bit of flour. Use a rolling pin to roll each puff pastry sheet out and lightly smooth the surface.

2. Cut the puff pastry into quarters to fit into each section of your waffle maker.

3. Place a piece of puff pastry in the four sections of the waffle maker and cook for about 5 minutes or until crisp. Repeat with the rest of the puff pastry.

4. Toss sugar with 1 teaspoon of cinnamon in a medium mixing bowl.

5.   When the waffles are done remove them from the waffle maker and place them one by one into the cinnamon sugar; toss to coat.

6.   Remove from the cinnamon sugar and cut each waffle into four long strips to resemble mini churros.

7.   Make the Mexican chocolate dipping sauce by heating the cream, over medium-high heat, in a metal saucepan until the cream is hot - but not boiling.

8.   Whisk in the chocolate chips and continue to whisk until chocolate is melted.

9.   Add cinnamon, ancho chili and salt and whisk until well-incorporated.

10.   Transfer to a bowl and serve alongside the waffle churros for dipping fun.

Nutritional Info: Calories: 1015 | Sodium: 359| Dietary Fiber: 2.4 g | Total Fat: 65.8 g | Total Carbs: 102.0 g | Protein: 11.6 g.

Ham & Cheese Waffles

Servings: 1 | Prep Time: 5 minutes | Cook Time: 5 minutes

When it comes to snacking nothing is better than a hot ham and cheese—except when it's waffled! Serve up this savory little snack mid-day to curb your cravings and keep you on a healthy lifestyle track.

Ingredients

2 slices of bread, like Ezekiel Sesame Bread or Hawaiian Style Bread

1 tablespoon softened butter, for brushing

6 slices deli thin ham, like Black Forest or Honey Ham

2 slices vermont cheddar cheese

Instructions

1. Preheat the waffle maker.

2. Generously butter one side of each slice of bread. Lay the bread, butter side down on a plate. Top one slice of bread with a slice of cheese.

3. Pile the ham on top of the cheese and top ham with another piece of cheese. Lay the other slice of bread on top of the ham butter side up.

4. Open the waffle iron, hold the sandwich together and carefully invert it so the buttered top is facing down on the waffle iron.

5. Cook the sandwich about 5 minutes or until the cheese is melted and bubbling out or the bread is golden browned.

6. Use tongs or a spatula to carefully remove the sandwich from the waffle iron and transfer it to a cutting board. Cut in half (or quarters) and serve piping hot.

Nutritional Info: Calories: 435 | Sodium: 1764| Dietary Fiber: 1.7 g | Total Fat: 27.7 g | Total Carbs: 13.6 g | Protein: 31.8 g.

Mac N' Cheese Waffles

Servings: 4 | Prep Time: 40 minutes | Cook Time: 10 minutes

Turn your favorite comfort dish into a comforting waffle with this simple, easy recipe. If you love mac n' cheese, these waffles are packed with a gooey center that will transform the way your afternoon snack in no time. Serve them up as a side dish or cut into fours as mac n' cheese waffle bites.

Ingredients

1 package macaroni and cheese, like Annie's or Kraft (alternatively homemade)

1 cup cheddar cheese, shredded

Non-stick cooking spray

Instructions

1. Cook macaroni and cheese as per the directions on the box.

2. Pour into a rimmed baking sheet and refrigerate for 30 minutes.

3. Preheat the waffle maker.

4. Remove mac n' cheese from refrigerator and slice into four 7 inch squares; big enough to fit in the waffle maker, but not fall out the sides.

5. Spray both griddles of the waffle maker with non-stick cooking spray.

6. Place one slice of mac n' cheese on the waffle iron. Top it with a generous amount of shredded cheese in the center of the slice. Add a second slice of mac n' cheese and close the waffle maker lid.

7. Set the timer for 3 minutes. Flip the waffle maker over. Cook for about 2 -3 minutes or until the cheese is melted and bubbling out or the waffle is golden browned.

8.   Remove and repeat with second waffle.

9.   Serve while piping hot and gooey!

Nutritional Info: Calories: 321 | Sodium: 1236| Dietary Fiber: 1.3 g | Total Fat: 15.6 g | Total Carbs: 29.4 g | Protein: 15.5 g.

Mashed Potato Waffle

Servings: 4 | Prep Time: 15 minutes | Cook Time: 10 minutes

Turn your favorite comfort food into waffle heaven with this yummy recipe. Mashed Potato Waffles are absolutely amazing on their own. Serve them up with a side salad or lean protein to make a hearty meal. No matter which way you eat them, they're sure to warm your waffle loving heart.

Ingredients

4 tablespoons unsalted butter

1/4 cup buttermilk

2 large eggs

2 cups leftover mashed potatoes

3 tablespoons chives, chopped

1/2 cup all-purpose flour

1/2 teaspoon baking powder

1/4 teaspoon baking soda

1/2 teaspoon sea salt

1/2 teaspoon fresh ground black pepper

1/4 teaspoon garlic powder

1 cup grated cheddar cheese

Sour cream, for garnish

Instructions

1. Grease and preheat the Cuisinart Belgian Waffle Maker.

2. Melt butter in a small saucepan over medium-low heat.

3. Whisk in buttermilk and eggs until thoroughly combined.

4. Add the leftover mashed potatoes, cheddar cheese and 2 tablespoons of the chives; gently stir to combine.

5. In a small mixing bowl, whisk together flour, baking powder, baking soda, salt, pepper, and garlic powder.

6. Fold the dry ingredients into the wet ingredients. Mix with a spoon until all of the flour is well-combined; try not to overmix the batter.

7. Spoon 1/4 cup batter into the waffle maker.

8. Cook the waffle for 2 - 3 minutes or until the steam has ceased.

9. Garnish with a dollop of sour cream and remaining chives.

Nutritional Info: Calories: 369 | Sodium: 627| Dietary Fiber: 2.4 g | Total Fat: 23.8 g | Total Carbs: 25.7 g | Protein: 13.8 g.

Quesaffles

Servings: 2 | Prep Time: 10 minutes | Cook Time: 5 minutes

When it comes to getting the most out of your Cuisinart Belgian Waffle Maker, these melt in your mouth waffled quesadillas will put a smile on anyone's face. Perfect for an afternoon snack or meal on the go, Quaffles combine the best of both worlds with a fun, hearty snack that is out of this world.

Ingredients

1 tablespoon olive oil

2 poblano peppers in chipotle sauce, drained and thinly sliced

1 serrano pepper, seeded and diced

4 flour tortillas

1 1/2 cups pepper jack cheese, shredded

2 teaspoons taco seasoning mix

Sour cream, for topping

Salsa, for topping

Cilantro, for topping

Instructions

1. Heat a small skillet on medium heat. Add the olive oil followed by the poblano and serrano peppers.

2. Cook for 2-3 minutes; until they just start to soften. Season the peppers with a small pinch of salt.

3. Cut tortillas to fit the waffle iron, if necessary.

4. Place a tortilla on the waffle iron and add a small amount of cheese, followed by about half of the pepper mix. Sprinkle tortilla with an even layer of taco seasoning and another good handful of cheese.

5. Top with a second tortilla and close the waffle iron.

6.   Cook the quesadilla until the cheese is melted and bubbling out or the tortilla is lightly browned.

7.   Remove quesadilla using a fork or plastic spatula. Cut into quarters for easy serving. Garnish with sour cream, salsa, and cilantro.

Nutritional Info: Calories: 886 | Sodium: 1235| Dietary Fiber: 3.8 g | Total Fat: 65.4 g | Total Carbs: 27.4 g | Protein: 47.9 g.

Strawberry Jam Grilled Cheese Waffles

Servings: 1 | Prep Time: 5 minutes | Cook Time: 5 minutes

The perfect afternoon or after school snack, these scrumptious waffle sandwiches are just the thing to curb before dinner cravings. Of course, they can also be made into a meal with a side of carrot sticks or apple slices for savory, sweet, healthy lunch or dinner.

Ingredients

2 tablespoons salted butter

2 slices sourdough bread

2 slices white vermont cheddar cheese

1 tablespoon strawberry jam

Instructions

1. Preheat the waffle maker.

2. Spread butter on one side of each slice of bread. Lay the bread on a plate, butter-side down.

3. Top each slice of bread with a thin layer of strawberry jam. Then lay a thin piece of cheddar on each slice.

4. Sandwich the pieces together and lay it onto the Cuisinart Belgian Waffle Maker.

5. Cook for 4 minutes or until the edges are browned and crispy and the cheese is melted.

Nutritional Info: Calories: 690 | Sodium: 927| Dietary Fiber: 1.5 g | Total Fat: 42.8 g | Total Carbs: 55.5 g | Protein: 21.7 g.

Waffle Pops

Servings: 6 - 8 | Prep Time: 30 minutes | Cook Time: 15 minutes

Get the afternoon party started with delicious, spicy Caribbean Shrimp Stuffed Waffle Pops. Waffle pops are quick and easy to make and are an absolutely delicious midday snack or served as party food!

Ingredients

3/4 cups yellow cornmeal

3/4 cups all-purpose flour

1 tablespoon caribbean seasoning

1 teaspoon sugar or sugar substitute

1 1/2 teaspoons baking powder

1 (16-ounce) can of beer

1 tablespoon half and half

1 egg

1 pound shrimp, deveined and cooked

1 tablespoon olive oil

Wooden skewers

Non-stick cooking spray

Instructions

1. Add the egg and half and half to a large mixing bowl; whisk until well-blended.

2. Add the cornmeal, flour, 1 tablespoon caribbean seasoning, sugar, and baking powder.

3. Slowly whisk beer into the mixture to make the batter. Mixture should be fairly thick, but add a little more half and half if needed. Mix in jalapeño and onion.

4. Lightly spray the waffle iron with nonstick cooking spray.

5. Sprinkle remaining 1 tablespoon of caribbean seasoning onto the shrimp. Place a wooden skewer in each shrimp.

6.   Dip four skewers at a time into the waffle batter, then place each on one of the four quarters of the waffle maker.

7.   Cook about 2-3 minutes or until waffle pops are golden and crispy on the outside. Repeat until all waffle pops are done.

8.   Serve with cocktail sauce or hot sauce!

Nutritional Info: Calories: 204 | Sodium: 154| Dietary Fiber: 1.2 g | Total Fat: 4.0 g | Total Carbs: 21.7 g | Protein: 16.1 g.

Waffled Pineapple with Chili Powder

Servings: 2 | Prep Time: 3 minutes | Cook Time: 5 minutes

Turn ordinary snacks into something spectacular with the Cuisinart Belgian Waffle Maker. Sweet pineapple really kicks a punch when waffled with chili powder. Serve it on its own or with a slice of ham for some protein loading fun!

Ingredients

1 can sliced pineapple in juice

Non-stick cooking spray

Ancho chili powder, for dusting

Instructions

1. Preheat the waffle maker and coat both sides of the waffle maker griddle with nonstick spray.

2. Open the can and drain the juice from the pineapple.

3. Set the sliced pineapple on a plate covered with paper towels and blot the slices dry.

4. Place the slices of pineapple, in an even layer, on the waffle maker and close the lid. Flip the waffle maker over.

5. Cook for 1 minute before checking. When the pineapple is starting to show golden brown waffle indentations, remove it and place it on a paper towel lined plate.

6. Dust the pineapple with chili powder and serve.

Nutritional Info: Calories: 197 | Sodium: 33| Dietary Fiber: 3.2 g | Total Fat: 0.0 g | Total Carbs: 52.4 g | Protein: 0.0 g.

Waffled Pudding

Servings: 6 | Prep Time: 10 minutes | Cook Time: 10 minutes

Turn snack time into an amazing adventure with Waffled Pudding. Yep, you read that right - you can waffle pudding in your Cuisinart Belgian Waffle Maker. Serve as a delicious afternoon snack or as a decadent dessert with a side of butter pecan

Ingredients

1 3/4 cups unbleached flour

1 teaspoon baking powder

1 teaspoon cinnamon

1/2 teaspoon nutmeg

1/4 teaspoon sea salt

2 teaspoons pure vanilla extract

1 3/4 cups 2% milk

1/2 cup coconut oil

2 eggs, separated

For the custard:

2 cups heavy cream

2 cups half and half

6 large egg yolks

1/2 cup brown sugar

2 teaspoons salt

Instructions

1. Combine dry ingredients in large mixing bowl. Stir until well-blended.

2. In a separate mixing bowl, combine all of the liquid ingredients - except the egg whites.

3. Incorporate the wet ingredients into the dry ingredients, stirring until just combined.

4. Whip the egg whites until they form soft peaks, then fold them into the batter.

5. Fill the waffle iron with 3/4 cups of batter.

6. Cook for 2 - 3 minutes or until golden and fluffy.

7. Transfer to a cooling rack.

8. Prepare the custard by combining all of the ingredients in a large mixing bowl until well-blended.

9. Break the waffles into 1 inch pieces and submerge into the custard. Set aside to soak for 5 minutes.

10. Repeat steps 5 through 8 until all waffle bread pudding is used.

11. Serve warm with your favorite ice cream or simply smothered in syrup.

Nutritional Info: Calories: 695 | Sodium: 969| Dietary Fiber: 1.2 g | Total Fat: 50.1 g | Total Carbs: 49.4 g | Protein: 13.9 g.

Winter Squash Waffle

Servings: 2 | Prep Time: 5 minutes | Cook Time: 10 minutes

Get creative with winter squash and waffle it for one super-healthy snack that is out of this world! Glazed with chipotle maple syrup, this snack is savory and sweet. It's also so quick and easy, you'll wonder why you never tried it before!

Ingredients

1 winter squash, thin sliced

Non-stick cooking spray

3 teaspoons chipotle chili powder

1/4 cup maple syrup

Instructions

1. Preheat the waffle maker and coat both sides of the waffle maker griddle with nonstick spray.

2. Set the sliced winter squash on a plate covered with paper towels and blot the slices dry.

3. Place the slices of pineapple, in an even layer, on the waffle maker and close the lid. Flip the waffle maker over.

4. Cook for 5 minutes before checking. When the squash is starting to show golden brown waffle indentations, remove it and place it on a paper towel lined plate.

5. Heat the maple syrup in a small saucepan on low-medium heat. Whisk in the chipotle powder until well-incorporated.

6. Glaze the waffled winter squash and transfer to a cookie rack to cool. Enjoy when glaze sets!

Nutritional Info: Calories: 201 | Sodium: 49| Dietary Fiber: 4.6 g | Total Fat: 0.9 g | Total Carbs: 51.0 g | Protein: 2.2 g.

9

Dessert Waffles

Apple Pie Waffles

Servings: 2 | Prep Time: 10 minutes | Cook Time: 10 minutes

Turn the American favorite dessert into a delectable waffle for one amazing treat. Serve these tasty waffles alongside a scoop of vanilla ice cream for one sinfully sweet a la mode ending to any meal.

Ingredients

1 1/2 cups all-purpose flour

3 teaspoons baking powder

2 tablespoons sugar

1 teaspoon salt

1/2 teaspoon cinnamon

Pinch nutmeg

1 1/2 cups milk

1 egg

1 tablespoon olive oil

1 teaspoon pure vanilla extract

1 small apple, chopped into small cubes

For Apple Pie Center:

1 apple, sliced

2 tablespoons unsalted butter

1 tablespoon sugar or sugar substitute

1/4 teaspoon cinnamon

Pure maple syrup, for topping

Instructions

1.   Preheat the waffle maker.

2.   Preheat the oven to 200 degrees Fahrenheit to keep the waffles warm before serving.

3. Whisk together the flour, baking powder, sugar, salt, cinnamon, and nutmeg in a large mixing bowl.

4. Make a well in the center of the dry ingredients and add the milk, egg, olive oil, and vanilla. Whisk together until fully incorporated and smooth.

5. Fold in the chopped apples.

6. Lightly grease the waffle maker with olive oil.

7. Carefully pour half of the batter into the middle of the waffle maker.

8. Cook until the edges are brown and crispy, about 5 minutes; repeat with the remaining batter.

9. Place the waffles in the oven to stay warm while making the apple pie filling.

10. Melt the butter in a small saucepan. Add the sliced apples and sprinkle with the sugar and cinnamon. Cook until the apples are soft and a glaze has started to form, about 5-7 minutes.

11. Cut the large waffles into 4 small squares. Place the apple pie filling on top of four of the waffle squares and top with the remaining waffles.

12. Drizzle with maple syrup, serve immediately and enjoy!

Nutritional Info: Calories: 796 | Sodium: 1372| Dietary Fiber: 7.2 g | Total Fat: 25.8 g | Total Carbs: 126.1 g | Protein: 19.1 g.

Bacon Wonuts (Waffle Donuts)

Servings: 6-8 | Prep Time: 15 minutes | Cook Time: 20 minutes

Donut and bacon lovers rejoice - this recipe is for you! We've combined the best of both worlds to bring you a waffle that will knock your savory and sweet socks off. Perfect for dessert, this sweet little wonut can be cut into fours and served as mini-desserts for any fun night in too.

Ingredients

For the waffles:

3/4 cups sugar	2 eggs
4 teaspoons baking powder	1/4 cup unsalted butter, melted
1 1/2 teaspoons salt	1 cup buttermilk or milk
1/2 teaspoon nutmeg	3 cups unbleached flour

For the maple glaze:

3/4 cups maple syrup	8 strips of cooked bacon, chopped into pieces for topping
4 tablespoons unsalted butter	
1/2 cup powdered sugar	

Instructions

1. Mix the sugar, baking powder, salt, and nutmeg in a large mixing bowl.
2. Add in the eggs, milk, and melted butter to the bowl and mix until well-incorporated.

3.   Add in the flour and mix until thoroughly combined. The batter will be thick and have a bit of a dough consistency. If it is too dough-like, feel free to add some more milk, tablespoon by tablespoon, until the batter is easier to work with.

4.   Preheat the waffle maker.

5.   Pour one 1/2 cup of batter into the waffle griddle and set the timer for 5 - 6 minutes.

6.   Close the waffle maker lid. grasp both handles and flip the waffle maker over 180°. Cook until no steam rises from the waffle maker or the timer goes off.

7.   Make the glaze by heating the maple syrup and unsalted butter on the stove on low heat in a saucepan; stir continuously until the butter has completely melted.

8.   Remove the glaze from the heat and fold in the powdered sugar.

9.   Set the glaze aside to cool down. Pour over the waffles. Sprinkle the crumbled bacon pieces on top of the waffles and serve.

Nutritional Info: Calories: 633 | Sodium: 1228| Dietary Fiber: 1.4 g | Total Fat: 25.3 g | Total Carbs: 85.0 g | Protein: 17.9 g.

Carrot Cake Waffles

Servings: 2 | Prep Time: 5 minutes | Cook Time: 10 minutes

Turn decadent carrot cake into a waffle dessert with this tastefully sweet recipe. The best part about this delicious recipe is that it can be modified to fit any gluten-free lifestyle. You'll fall in love with these delicious waffles no matter which way you like to make them!

Ingredients

1/2 cup all-purpose or gluten-free flour

1/2 teaspoon cinnamon

1/4 teaspoon salt

1/4 teaspoon baking soda

1 teaspoon baking powder

2 tablespoons pure maple syrup

1/4 cup carrot, shredded

1/3 cup milk

1 tablespoon olive oil

1 teaspoon pure vanilla extract

Cream cheese frosting, for drizzling

Instructions

1. Preheat the waffle maker.
2. Combine first 6 ingredients in a large mixing bowl, and stir until well-combined.
3. In a separate mixing bowl, combine remaining ingredients.
4. Grease your waffle maker with non-stick cooking spray.
5. Incorporate wet ingredients into the dry, and stir to make a batter.
6. Pour half of the batter into the center of the waffle maker.
7. Set the timer for 2 - 3 minutes and cook until golden fluffy; repeat with remaining batter.

8. Frost each carrot cake waffle with cream cheese frosting and serve.

Nutritional Info: Calories: 262 | Sodium: 483| Dietary Fiber: 1.6 g | Total Fat: 8.2 g | Total Carbs: 42.5 g | Protein: 4.7 g.

Chocolate Waffle Cookies

Servings: 8 | Prep Time: 15 minutes | Cook Time: 20 minutes

For the chocolate waffle lover, these cookies are just the thing to quench your decadent sweet tooth! Sinfully sweet, these little devils are quick and easy too.

Ingredients

3 ounces dark cacao chocolate, coarsely chopped

2 1/4 sticks unsalted butter

4 large eggs

1 teaspoon pure vanilla extract

1 1/2 cups granulated sugar

1/2 teaspoon coarse salt

1 1/2 teaspoons ground cinnamon

1/2 cup cocoa powder, plus 2 tablespoons for icing

1 1/2 cups all-purpose flour

1/4 cup confectioner's sugar, plus more for dusting

1 1/2 tablespoons 2% milk

Non-stick cooking spray

Instructions

1. Preheat the waffle maker.

2. Melt chocolate with 2 sticks of butter in a medium saucepan over medium-high heat; stir constantly. Let cool slightly.

3. Add eggs, vanilla, and granulated sugar to a medium mixing bowl. Use an electric mixer fitted with the paddle attachment and mix on medium speed, 4 - 5 minutes, until pale.

4. Fold in chocolate mixture, salt, cinnamon, 1/2 cup cocoa powder, and the flour.

5. Lightly coat the Cuisinart waffle grids with non-stick cooking spray.

6. Spoon 1 tablespoon batter onto center of each waffle maker.

7. Melt the remaining 2 tablespoons of butter in a small saucepan over low heat. Add confectioners' sugar and remaining 2 tablespoons cocoa powder; stir until smooth.

8. Stir in milk.

9. Gently dip 1 surface of each cookie in icing so that just the waffle lines are coated; repeat with remaining cookies.

10. Transfer to wire racks, icing side up, and let stand until set, about 10 minutes.

11. Dust iced surfaces of cookies with confectioners' sugar and enjoy!

Nutritional Info: Calories: 577 | Sodium: 349| Dietary Fiber: 2.8 g | Total Fat: 32.4 g | Total Carbs: 69.2 g | Protein: 7.7 g.

Cupcake Waffles

Servings: 6 - 8 | Prep Time: 15 minutes | Cook Time: 15 minutes

Turn your Cuisinart Belgian Waffle Maker into something super special and whip up some delicious little cupcake waffles. This recipe is amazing because you can use any cake your waffle loving heart desires.

Ingredients

1 box devil's food cake mix

1 cup water

1/3 cup vegetable oil

3 eggs

Non-stick cooking spray

For the Icing:

1 (16-ounce) package of dark chocolate icing

1 (8-ounce) package of cream cheese, softened

Sprinkles, for topping

Instructions

1. Whisk together the cake mix, water, oil, and eggs in a large mixing bowl until well combined.

2. Drop 1/2 cup of the cake batter into the waffle maker. Cook for 2 -3 minutes or until golden and fluffy. Repeat for remaining cake batter.

3. Use a hand blender to mix the cream cheese and icing together.

4. Cut the waffles into 4 pieces. Top one piece with icing, layer with a second waffle and top with icing and sprinkles; repeat until all cupcakes are assembled and enjoy!

Nutritional Info: Calories: 785 | Sodium: 588| Dietary Fiber: 2.5 g | Total Fat: 44.6 g | Total Carbs: 85.7 g | Protein: 11.5 g.

Glazed Waffle Cookies

Servings: 10-13 | Prep Time: 10 minutes | Cook Time: 10 minutes

Simply sweet iced cookies are the perfect thing to go with your after dinner cup of joe. Add them to a lunch box for a little surprise treat, or just whip them up when you're craving something on the sweet side of life.

Ingredients

1/2 cup unsalted butter, softened

1/2 cup granulated sugar

1/4 cup packed brown sugar or brown sugar substitute

1 large egg

1 teaspoon pure vanilla extract

1 1/4 cups all-purpose flour

1/4 teaspoon baking soda

3/4 teaspoons cinnamon

1/4 teaspoon salt

For the Icing:

1 (2-ounce) package cream cheese or neufchatel, softened

1/3 cup powdered sugar

1/2 teaspoon vanilla

1/2 cup heavy cream or milk

Cinnamon powder, for dusting

Instructions

1. Whip butter and sugars together, in a large mixing bowl, until light and fluffy.

2. Stir in egg and vanilla. Slowly incorporate dry ingredients until well-incorporated.

3.   Preheat the waffle maker.

4.   Spray both sides of the griddle with nonstick cooking spray.

5.   Scoop 1 tablespoon of cookie dough into balls until all dough is rolled. Place one dough ball into each of the four quarters of the waffle maker.

6.   Set the timer for 2 minutes.

7.   Remove cookies and transfer to a cooling rack; repeat until all cookies are waffled.

8.   For the icing: mix cream cheese, sugar and vanilla together in a large mixing bowl until smooth.

9.   Slowly stir in milk or heavy cream to create a glaze.

10.   Drizzle icing over the waffle cookies and top with more cinnamon to serve.

Nutritional Info: Calories: 196 | Sodium: 143| Dietary Fiber: 0.0 g | Total Fat: 10.8 g | Total Carbs: 23.1 g | Protein: 2.2 g.

Red Velvet Waffles

Servings: 5 - 6 | Prep Time: 5 minutes | Cook Time: 10 minutes

Red velvet cake has never been so delicious - why not waffle it!? The Cuisinart Belgian Waffle Maker is perfect for taking this classic cake one step further and turning it into dessert heaven.

Ingredients

2 cups all-purpose flour	1 3/4 cups buttermilk
3 tablespoons granulated sugar	1/3 cup unsalted butter, melted and cooled
1 tablespoon unsweetened cocoa powder	2 teaspoons pure vanilla extract
4 teaspoons baking powder	1/2 teaspoon white distilled vinegar
3/4 teaspoons sea salt	2 teaspoons red food coloring
2 eggs	Non-stick cooking spray

For Cream Cheese Icing:

6 ounces cream cheese, softened	2 cups powdered sugar
6 tablespoons butter, softened	1 teaspoon vanilla extract
	1/2 cup – 1 cup whole milk

Instructions

1. Whisk together the flour, sugar, cocoa powder, baking powder, and salt. Set aside.

2. Grease the Cuisinart Belgian Waffle Maker with non-stick cooking spray and preheat.

3. In a medium mixing bowl, beat together the eggs, buttermilk, butter, vanilla, and vinegar on the lowest speed until well-combined.

4. Add 1 teaspoon red food coloring to the batter.

5. Pour milk mixture into dry ingredients and still until well-combined. If the batter is light red, add additional food coloring and mix gently.

6. Pour 3/4 cups batter into the waffle maker.

7. Cook the waffle for 2 - 3 minutes or until golden and fluffy; repeat until all batter is used.

8. For the cream cheese icing: Beat the cream cheese and butter with a hand mixer until fluffy.

9. Gradually fold in the powdered sugar.

10. Add wet ingredients, alternating with the milk and vanilla; start with 1/2 cup milk and add more to achieve desired consistency.

11. Glaze waffles and serve!

Nutritional Info: Calories: 706 | Sodium: 589| Dietary Fiber: 1.5 g | Total Fat: 35.6 g | Total Carbs: 86.1 g | Protein: 12.4 g.

Waffle Brownies

Servings: 4 | Prep Time: 10 minutes | Cook Time: 15 minutes

Turn ooey, gooey brownies into delicious waffles with this easy recipe. Waffle Brownies are a sweet way to transform dessert into fun. Top them with ice cream and hot fudge for one truly decadent dessert, or go fresh and healthy with whipped cream and fresh fruit for a clean healthy dessert.

Ingredients

6 ounces bittersweet chocolate

1 stick butter, unsalted and melted

2 large eggs

1 cup sugar or 1/2 cup sugar substitute

2 tablespoons unsweetened cocoa powder

1 teaspoon pure vanilla extract

1 teaspoon espresso powder or finely ground espresso

1/2 teaspoon sea salt

2 cups unbleached flour

Non-stick cooking spray

Fresh berries, optional topping

Whipped cream

Vanilla ice cream, optional topping

Hot fudge, optional topping

Instructions

1. Preheat the waffle maker.

2. Fill a saucepan with one-inch water and bring to a simmer. Melt the chocolate in a glass or heatproof bowl by placing it in the mouth of the pot; stir frequently until melted and fully combined. Remove from heat and allow to cool.

3. Combine the melted butter, sugar, and vanilla in a large mixing bowl. Beat in the eggs, one at a time, mixing well after each, until thoroughly blended.

4. Fold in the melted chocolate.

5. Sift the flour, cocoa powder, and salt into the bowl and gradually stir flour mixture into the egg mixture until blended.

6. Grease the waffle maker with non-stick cooking spray. Pour just enough batter into the waffle maker to cover the griddle. Set the timer for 2 minutes.

7. Close the waffle maker lid. Set the timer and grasp both handles and flip the waffle maker over 180°.

8. When the timer goes off the waffle brownies are done. Repeat until all batter is used.

9. Top with your favorite dessert toppings and enjoy!

Nutritional Info: Calories: 890 | Sodium: 467| Dietary Fiber: 4.0 g | Total Fat: 39.0 g | Total Carbs: 124.8 g | Protein: 13.6 g.

Waffle Ice Cream Sandwich

Servings: 8 | Prep Time: 15 minutes | Cook Time: 20 minutes

Cuisinart Belgian Waffle Maker is perfect for fresh, homemade ice cream sandwiches. Whip some up on a hot summer day and stuff them with your favorite treats for loads of waffle fun.

Ingredients

2 cups all-purpose flour

3/4 cups sugar or sugar substitute

3 1/2 teaspoons baking powder

2 large eggs, separated

1 1/2 cups milk

1 cup unsalted butter, melted

1 teaspoon pure vanilla extract

2 pints vanilla ice cream strawberry jam

Instructions

1. Preheat the waffle maker.
2. Combine flour, sugar and baking powder in a mixing bowl.
3. In a second mixing bowl, lightly beat the egg yolks.
4. Fold the milk, butter and vanilla into the egg yolks and mix well.
5. Fold dry ingredients into the egg mixture until just combined.
6. Beat egg whites in a metal mixing bowl until stiff peaks form; fold into batter.
7. Pour approximately 3/4 to 1 cup of waffle batter into the center of the bottom waffle grid until covered, but not leaking over the side.
8. Set the Cuisinart timer by pressing the minutes and seconds buttons to the desired time.

9. repeat until all waffles are cooked.

10. Cut individual waffles into 4 quarters.

11. Cut a slit down the side of the ice cream container. Peel away the container until you are left with only the ice cream.

12. Lay the ice cream on its side and with a sharp knife, slice it into four 1/2 inch rounds.

13. Assemble the sandwiches with a tablespoon of strawberry jam on top of the waffle. Add a slice of ice cream. Top with a second waffle and enjoy!

Nutritional Info: Calories: 577 | Sodium: 263| Dietary Fiber: 1.4 g | Total Fat: 33.4 g | Total Carbs: 63.1 g | Protein: 9.1 g.

Waffled Cheesecake with Berry Syrup

Servings: 6 - 8 | Prep Time: 15 minutes | Cook Time: 15 minutes

Cheesecake lovers will fall head over heels when they whip up this quick and easy Waffled Cheesecake with Berry Syrup. Packed full of savory flavor and topped with sweet berry syrup - this one is great for any meal or snack time of the day.

Ingredients

*Waffle batter [**See True Belgian Waffle Recipe on page 58**]*

4 ounces cream cheese, softened

1/4 cup sour cream, room temperature

1 tablespoon milk, room temperature

1 medium egg

2 tablespoons sugar

Berry Syrup:

1 cup frozen mixed berries

1 tablespoon lemon juice

1/3 cup maple syrup

Instructions

1. Add the frozen berries and lemon juice to a small saucepan and heat over medium-low heat; let cook for about 15 minutes, or until berries have broken down.

2. Stir in maple syrup and set aside.

3. While the berry syrup is cooking, start the cheesecake waffles.

4. Whisk together the cream cheese, sour cream, milk, egg, and sugar in a medium mixing bowl and set aside.

5. Prepare the waffle batter according to the recipe above.

6. Preheat the waffle maker.

7. When waffle maker is ready, layer the batter with 1/3 cup waffle batter, then 1/4 cup cheesecake batter on top, then 1/3 cup waffle batter on top of that batter.

8. Cook for 3-4 minutes or until golden and fluffy; repeat until batter is finished and all waffles are cooked.

9. Top waffles with sugar-free syrup and serve warm.

Nutritional Info: Calories: 130 | Sodium: 56| Dietary Fiber: 0.6 g | Total Fat: 7.1 g | Total Carbs: 14.8 g | Protein: 2.2 g.

10

Clean Eating, Paleo & Gluten-Free Waffles

Banana Quinoa Waffles

Servings: 6 | Prep Time: 10 minutes | Cook Time: 5 minutes

Eat clean and healthy when it comes to using your Cuisinart Belgian Waffle Maker - anything is possible. Even scrumptious banana waffles!

Ingredients

1/2 cup brown rice flour

1/2 cup toasted quinoa flour

1/2 cup tapioca starch

1 teaspoon baking powder

1/2 teaspoon cinnamon

1/4 teaspoon nutmeg

1/8 teaspoon salt

1 ripe banana, mashed

2 eggs, separated - 1 yolk + 2 whites

1 1/2 cups almond milk

1 teaspoon pure vanilla extract

Non-stick cooking spray

Sugar free syrup, for topping

Fresh fruit, for topping

Yogurt, for topping

Instructions

1. Preheat the waffle maker.
2. Combine the flours, baking powder, spices and salt in a large mixing bowl and set aside.
3. Combine the banana, egg yolk, milk and vanilla in a separate mixing bowl and beat until smooth.
4. In a third mixing bowl, beat the egg whites using a hand mixer until stiff peaks form.
5. Add the wet ingredients to the dry and gently stir together with a wooden spoon until just combined; do not overmix.
6. Gently fold the egg whites into the batter until just incorporated.

7. Lightly grease your waffle maker with non-stick cooking spray, and pour a scoop of the batter into the bottom and close the lid.

8. Flip the waffle maker over.

9. Cook about 2 - 3 minutes or until light golden. Repeat with remaining waffle batter.

10. Top with fresh fruit, yogurt, sugar free syrup or whatever toppings your heart desires. Go wild with these waffles!

Nutritional Info: Calories: 410 | Sodium: 121| Dietary Fiber: 4.0 g | Total Fat: 24.4 g | Total Carbs: 44.9 g | Protein: 6.6 g.

Choco Protein Waffles

Servings: 2 | Prep Time: 5 minutes | Cook Time: 10 minutes

Breakfast just got super-clean with these gluten-free waffles bursting with chocolate. Top with a dairy-free whipped cream to keep it Paleo or simply enjoy with your favorite syrup for some waffle fun.

Ingredients

1/2 cup hemp protein

1/4 cup arrowroot

1/4 cup cocoa powder

1/2 teaspoon baking soda

1 teaspoon cinnamon powder

1/3 cup mashed banana

1/2 cup coconut milk

1 tablespoon sugar or sugar substitute

Instructions

1. Place all dry ingredients into a bowl and mix together.
2. Fold in the mashed banana stevia and milk. Beat with a hand mixer until batter is well-incorporated and slightly thick.
3. Scoop 3/4 cups batter into the waffle maker.
4. Close the waffle maker lid. Set the timer for 3 minutes. Flip the waffle maker over.
5. Cook until golden and fluffy.
6. Transfer waffle to a plate and tent with aluminum foil to keep warm; continue to cook waffles until all of the batter is used.
7. Serve plain or with your favorite syrup!

Nutritional Info: Calories: 482 | Sodium: 330| Dietary Fiber: 13.7 g | Total Fat: 21.6 g | Total Carbs: 33.6 g | Protein: 47.1 g.

High Protein Zucchini Waffles

Servings: 2 | Prep Time: 5 minutes | Cook Time: 10 minutes

Pack in a full serving of protein and veggies at breakfast with these delicious, melt in your mouth waffles! High Protein Zucchini Waffles are just the way to jump start your day.

Ingredients

- 3/4 cups spelt flour
- 1/2 cup "old-fashioned" or rolled oats, not instant
- 1/2 tablespoon baking powder
- 1/4 teaspoon sea salt
- 3/4 teaspoons cinnamon
- 6 ounces greek yogurt
- 1 large egg
- 1 tablespoon coconut oil, melted
- 1 tablespoon brown sugar or brown sugar substitute
- 1 teaspoon pure vanilla extract
- 1/2 cup zucchini, grated
- Non-stick cooking spray
- Sugar free syrup, for topping

Instructions

1. Preheat the waffle maker.
2. Combine the dry ingredients in a medium mixing bowl and sift together.
3. In a separate large mixing bowl, combine the wet ingredients until well-blended.
4. Fold the dry ingredients and mix until just combined; do not to over stir.
5. Scoop 3/4 cups batter into the waffle maker.

6.   Close the waffle maker lid. Set the timer for 3 minutes. Flip the waffle maker over.

7.   Cook until golden and fluffy; repeat with remaining batter until all waffles are cooked.

8.   Serve warm with your favorite sugar free syrup and enjoy.

Nutritional Info: Calories: 418 | Sodium: 340| Dietary Fiber: 8.4 g | Total Fat: 12.6 g | Total Carbs: 60.8 g | Protein: 17.2 g.

Mango Salsa Waffle

Servings: 4 | Prep Time: 15 minutes | Cook Time: 20 minutes

Master the clean eating revolution with this sublimely delicious Mango Salsa Waffle. Serve it up for breakfast with a fried egg or as a yummy lunch with a side salad - either way this waffle is the way to live the clean life!

Ingredients

For the waffles:

1/4 cup sweet rice flour

1/4 cup brown rice flour

1/2 cup oat flour

2 teaspoons baking powder

1 tablespoon sugar

1 teaspoon chili powder (optional)

1/2 teaspoon salt

3/4 cups almond milk (or regular milk)

2 tablespoons ground flax seed + 3 tablespoons extra milk

3 tablespoons melted coconut oil, or butter

For the Smoky Mango Avocado Salsa:

1 medium mango, peeled, pitted and diced

1 small avocado, peeled, pitted and diced

1 lime, juiced (about 2 tablespoons of fresh lime juice)

1/4 teaspoon salt

2 scallions, chopped

1/4 - 1/2 teaspoon ground smoked paprika

Pinch of red chili flakes

Instructions

1. Mix together the diced mango, avocado, lime juice, scallions, smoked paprika, red chili flakes and salt in a medium mixing bowl. Chill until ready to serve in the refrigerator.

2. Preheat the waffle maker.

3. Whisk together flour, baking powder, sugar, chili powder and salt in a mixing bowl.

4. In a small separate mixing bowl, whisk together the milk, flax and coconut oil.

5. Whisk the wet ingredients into the dry ingredients.

6. Pour one 1/2 cup batter into the waffle maker and set the timer for 3 minutes.

7. Close the waffle maker lid. Flip the waffle maker over. Cook until golden crisp.

8. Top each waffle with a generous spoonful of mango-avocado salsa and a fried egg, if desired. Add a pinch of salt and pepper on the top of each egg and serve.

Nutritional Info: Calories: 468 | Sodium: 460| Dietary Fiber: 8.2 g | Total Fat: 33.2 g | Total Carbs: 41.3 g | Protein: 5.9 g.

Potato Cheddar Waffles with Chives

Servings: 6 | Prep Time: 10 minutes | Cook Time: 10 minutes

When it comes to clean eating you can't ever have enough sides to match your lean protein and vegetables. For a super healthy way to add clean carbs to your diet, these waffles are absolutely out of this world.

Ingredients

4 tablespoons unsalted butter

1/4 cup kefir or almond milk

2 large eggs

2 cups mashed potatoes

3 tablespoons chopped chives

1/2 cup almond flour

1/2 teaspoon baking powder

1/4 teaspoon baking soda

1/2 teaspoon salt

1/2 teaspoon fresh ground black pepper

1/4 teaspoon garlic powder

1 cup vegan cheddar cheese shreds or your favorite cheese shredded

Salsa, for dipping

Instructions

1. Preheat the waffle maker.

2. Melt butter in a small saucepan over medium-low heat. As the butter melts it will begin to crackle and pop; continue to cook the butter until the crackling subsides and the butter begins to brown a bit. Immediately transfer the browned butter into a medium mixing bowl.

3. Whisk in kefir and eggs until thoroughly combined.

4. Add the mashed potatoes and 2 tablespoons chives; gently stir to combine.

5. In a separate small mixing bowl, whisk together flour, baking powder, baking soda, salt, pepper, and garlic powder.

6. Fold the dry ingredients to the wet ingredients until just combined.

7. Add 1/4 cup batter to the waffle maker.

8. Close the waffle maker lid. Set the timer for 2-3 minutes. Flip the waffle maker over.

9. Cook until golden on each side.

10. Remove waffles from the iron and place on a cooling rack.

11. Turn an oven to high broil. Place waffles on a baking sheet and top with cheddar cheese. Place waffles under the broiler until cheese is melted, about 30 seconds to 1 minute.

12. Remove from the oven, sprinkle with remaining chives and serve warm with a side of salsa for dipping!

Nutritional Info: Calories: 313 | Sodium: 742| Dietary Fiber: 0.0 g | Total Fat: 22.9 g | Total Carbs: 14.1 g | Protein: 13.6 g.

Pumpkin Cornbread Waffles

Servings: 4 | Prep Time: 15 minutes | Cook Time: 10 minutes

Serve up something decadently different with your Cuisinart Belgian Waffle Maker. Perfect with grilled shrimp au gratin, jambalaya, or covered in country gravy - these savory waffles will take on any flavor combination you can think of!

Ingredients

1/2 cup pumpkin puree

6 tablespoons unsalted butter, melted

1 cup cornmeal

3/4 cups all-purpose flour

1 tablespoon sugar

1 1/2 teaspoons baking powder

1/2 teaspoon baking soda

1/4 teaspoon sea salt 1 teaspoon allspice

2 large eggs, lightly beaten

1 1/2 cups buttermilk

Non-stick cooking spray

Instructions

1. Preheat and lightly grease the waffle maker with non-stick cooking spray.

2. Combine dry ingredients in a large mixing bowl; set aside.

3. Mix melted butter, buttermilk, and eggs in a separate mixing bowl; fold in the pumpkin.

4. Fold wet ingredients into the dry ingredients until a smooth batter forms.

5. Pour approximately 3/4 to 1 cup of waffle batter into the center of the bottom waffle grid until covered, but not leaking over the side.

6.   Set the Cuisinart timer by pressing the minutes and seconds buttons to the desired time.

7.   When the time has expired or you see no steam rising from the waffle maker, your waffle is done. Continue to cook waffles until all of the batter is used.

8.   Top with your favorite foods or enjoy on their own as an afternoon snack.

Nutritional Info: Calories: 446 | Sodium: 545| Dietary Fiber: 3.9 g | Total Fat: 22.0 g | Total Carbs: 52.6 g | Protein: 11.6 g.

Pumpkin Waffles

Servings: 4 | Prep Time: 10 minutes | Cook Time: 5 minutes

For the pumpkin lover at heart, these waffles are savory, sweet, and "oh so delicious" to eat! Treat yourself to something different when it comes to your morning routine.

Ingredients

1 cup pumpkin

1 1/2 cups unsweetened non-dairy milk, like almond or coconut

2 tablespoons maple syrup

2 tablespoons coconut oil, melted

2 tablespoons ground flax

2 cups oat flour

2 teaspoons baking powder

2 teaspoons cinnamon

1/4 teaspoon freshly grated nutmeg

1/2 teaspoon dried ground ginger

1/2 teaspoon cloves

Non-stick cooking spray

Butter, for topping (optional)

Maple syrup, for topping (optional)

Instructions

1. Combine the ground flax, oat flour, baking powder and spices in a medium mixing bowl.

2. Combine the pumpkin, milk, maple syrup and coconut oil in a separate mixing bowl.

3. Mix the wet ingredients into the dry to form a thick batter.

4. Spray both sides of the waffle maker griddle with non-stick cooking spray.

5. Scoop 1/3 cup of batter into the waffle iron.

6.   Cook 4 -5 minutes or until golden crisp; repeat until all waffles are cooked.

7.   Serve with a few pats of butter and maple syrup or generously top with your favorite waffle toppings.

Nutritional Info: Calories: 358 | Sodium: 51| Dietary Fiber: 8.0 g | Total Fat: 13.1 g | Total Carbs: 51.2 g | Protein: 10.4 g.

Quinoa Flour Waffles

Servings: 1 | Prep Time: 5 minutes | Cook Time: 5 minutes

If you love quinoa, these yummy waffles might be your favorite recipe yet! Of course, packed with loads of healthy protein - these waffles are also a great start to the day. Put a little jump in your morning routine and start the day right with a healthy meal.

Ingredients

1 egg beaten

1 ripe banana, mashed

3 tablespoons quinoa flour

1 teaspoon baking powder

2 tablespoons almond milk or 2%

Olive oil, for brushing

Instructions

1. Preheat the Cuisinart Belgian Waffle maker.
2. Whisk together the flour and baking powder in a mixing bowl; set aside.
3. Whisk together the banana, egg and milk in another mixing bowl.
4. Fold the banana mixture into the flour mixture until just combined.
5. Lightly brush the top and bottom of the waffle iron with oil.
6. Fill each section about three-quarters of the way full.
7. Cook until the waffles are golden brown, 4 to 6 minutes.
8. Serve with your favorite toppings!

Nutritional Info: Calories: 242 | Sodium: 72| Dietary Fiber: 3.8 g | Total Fat: 11.9 g | Total Carbs: 31.3 g | Protein: 7.5 g.

Spiced Sweet Potato Waffles

Servings: 1 | Prep Time: 5 minutes | Cook Time: 5 minutes

Spice up your life with these melt in your mouth waffles! Pumpkin spiced and everything nice is exactly what you might need with your morning cup of cold brew coffee.

Ingredients

1 medium sweet potato, peeled and spiralized	Nonstick cooking spray, like Pam Coconut Spray
1/2 teaspoon cinnamon	1 tablespoon maple syrup, for topping
1/2 teaspoon allspice	
1 medium egg	

Instructions

1. Preheat the waffle maker.
2. Heat a large skillet over medium heat and coat with cooking spray.
3. Add the sweet potato noodles to the skillet and cook for about 10 minutes, turning frequently, or until noodles have completely softened.
4. Add the noodles to a mixing bowl. Stir in the pumpkin spice and mix to combine thoroughly.
5. Fold in the egg and toss to combine until well-coated
6. Spray the waffle iron with cooking spray. Pack the noodles onto the waffle maker so that no noodles hang off the side and they fit in all of the grooves.
7. Close the waffle maker lid. Set the timer for 5 minutes, grasp both handles and flip the waffle maker over 180°.

8. When the time has expired or no steam rises from the waffle maker your waffle noodles are done.

9. Serve with maple syrup.

Nutritional Info: Calories: 171 | Sodium: 103| Dietary Fiber: 4.6 g | Total Fat: 4.7 g | Total Carbs: 25.6 g | Protein: 7.9 g.

Sugar-Free Waffle

Servings: 4 | Prep Time: 10 minutes | Cook Time: 15 minutes

You can be diabetic friendly with your Cuisinart Belgian Waffle Maker too! Serve this waffle with your favorite sugar-free syrup and a cup of black coffee for an amazing diabetic friendly meal option.

Ingredients

2 eggs, large

1 teaspoon pure vanilla extract

2 tablespoons coconut oil, partially melted

1 1/2 cups almond milk

1 cup gluten-free flour blend

1 teaspoon baking powder

1/2 teaspoon baking soda

2 teaspoons sugar substitute, like Splenda

Non-stick cooking spray

Instructions

1. Preheat your Cuisinart Belgian Waffle Maker and lightly grease with non-stick cooking spray.

2. Place dry ingredients into a large mixing bowl and combine. Add in the wet ingredients and mix until just combined; do not overmix.

3. Pour 1/2 cup of batter into the waffle maker.

4. Close the waffle maker lid. Set the timer for 5 minutes, grasp both handles and flip the waffle maker over 180°.

5. Cook for about 2-3 minutes or until golden and fluffy.

6. Serve with almond butter or fresh fruit.

Nutritional Info: Calories: 423 | Sodium: 205| Dietary Fiber: 2.8 g | Total Fat: 30.8 g | Total Carbs: 31.7 g | Protein: 8.1 g.

Sweet Potato Waffle Noodles

Servings: 1 | Prep Time: 5 minutes | Cook Time: 20 minutes

A super-sweet gluten-free treat, Sweet Potato Waffle Noodles are a great side dish to savory meat and veggies. Waffle noodles also make for a delicious main meal with parmesan cheese and butter, or can be served up as a clean afternoon snack.

Ingredients

1 medium sweet potato, peeled and spiralized

1/4 teaspoon salt

1/4 teaspoon pepper

1/4 teaspoon cinnamon

1 medium egg

Nonstick cooking spray, like Pam Coconut Spray

Instructions

1. Preheat the waffle maker.
2. Heat a large skillet over medium heat and coat with cooking spray.
3. Add the sweet potato noodles to the skillet and cook for about 10 minutes, turning frequently, or until noodles have completely softened.
4. Add the noodles to a mixing bowl. Stir in the spices and mix to combine thoroughly.
5. Fold in the egg and toss to combine until well-coated
6. Spray the waffle iron with cooking spray. Pack the noodles onto the waffle maker so that no noodles hang off the side and they fit in all of the grooves.
7. Close the waffle maker lid. Set the timer and flip the waffle maker over.

8.   Serve as a side dish with savory meat and grilled vegetables, or on their own with butter and shaved parmesan cheese!

Nutritional Info: Calories: 169 | Sodium: 684| Dietary Fiber: 4.2 g | Total Fat: 4.6 g | Total Carbs: 24.8 g | Protein: 7.9 g.

Vegan Waffles

Servings: 1 | Prep Time: 5 minutes | Cook Time: 5 minutes

Vegan, soy and gluten-free, these yummy waffles are just the thing to add to your Vegan or Vegetarian friendly diet. Full of nutritious and delicious ingredients, these waffles will melt in your clean living mouth.

Ingredients

1/4 cup oats

1/4 cup finely ground cornmeal

1/2 cup hazelnut milk

1/4 banana, sliced

2 dried medjool dates, sliced

1 teaspoon pure vanilla extract

1/4 teaspoon sea salt

1 teaspoon cinnamon

Non-stick cooking spray

Sliced fruit, for topping

Syrup, for topping

Instructions

1. Preheat the waffle maker.
2. Add all of the ingredients to a food processor. Process until well-mixed.
3. Spray the waffle maker with non-stick cooking spray.
4. Pour the batter into the preheated waffle maker.
5. Cook the waffle for 2 - 3 minutes or until the steam has ceased.
6. Serve hot with your favorite toppings like sliced bananas, sliced strawberries, maple syrup, or cinnamon & sugar.

Nutritional Info: Calories: 340 | Sodium: 539| Dietary Fiber: 7.6 g | Total Fat: 5.1 g | Total Carbs: 64.9 g | Protein: 10.0 g.

Waffled Apples

Servings: 2 - 4 | Prep Time: 5 minutes | Cook Time: 5 minutes

Baked apples are one clean and healthy way to snack. Paleo and Gluten-free friendly, these snacks are also perfect for Vegetarians and Vegans alike.

Ingredients

---

2 apples, your favorite variety   *Non-stick cooking spray*

Instructions

---

1. Preheat Cuisinart Belgian Waffle Maker.

2. Spray waffle maker with non-stick spray.

3. Place one apple slice in each section of the waffle maker.

4. Cook for about a minute or until the apples look waffled. Transfer to a paper towel lined plate to cool and repeat until all apples are waffled.

5. **Note: You can caramelize your apples by rubbing each slice with a little bit of sugar before you put them in the waffle maker.

Nutritional Info: Calories: 158 | Sodium: 0.0| Dietary Fiber: 9.8 g | Total Fat: 0.0 g | Total Carbs: 43.4 g | Protein: 0 g.

Waffled Fritters

Servings: 6 | Prep Time: 10 minutes | Cook Time: 10 minutes

Flavor filled fritters are just what every Paleo diet lover or clean eater will enjoy whipping something up when it comes to making the most out of your Cuisinart Belgian Waffle Maker. Packed with

Ingredients

4 cups zucchini, peeled and shredded

1/2 cup red bell pepper, thinly diced

3 tablespoons green onions, finely chopped

1 egg, lightly beaten

2 teaspoons soy sauce

1 teaspoon rice vinegar

1/4 teaspoon ground ginger

1 teaspoon salt

1 teaspoon black pepper

1/4 cup coconut flour

Non-stick cooking spray

Instructions

1. Preheat the waffle maker.

2. Combine and toss shredded zucchini, red bell pepper and green onions in a large mixing bowl; set aside.

3. Add the egg, soy sauce, rice vinegar, ground ginger, salt and pepper to a second mixing bowl and whisk until well-combined.

4. Pour egg mixture into zucchini mixture. Use your hands or a large wooden spoon to work the mixture until fully combined.

5. Fold in the coconut flour until all the liquid in the mixing bowl is absorbed.

6. Add 1/3 cup of the batter to the waffle maker.

7. Close the waffle maker lid. Set the timer for 2-3 minutes. Flip the waffle maker over.

8.   Cook until golden brown and serve hot!

Nutritional Info: Calories: 29 | Sodium: 506| Dietary Fiber: 1.2 g | Total Fat: 0.9 g |
Total Carbs: 3.7 g | Protein: 2.1 g.

Waffled Hash Browns

Servings: 2 | Prep Time: 10 minutes | Cook Time: 10 minutes

Waffled Hash Browns are a delicious addition to any breakfast, lunch, dinner or simply served as a mid-day snack. Quick and easy, you'll love this clean waffled dish.

Ingredients

1 russet potato, peeled

2 cups cold water

Salt and pepper to taste

Butter, for brushing waffle maker

Instructions

1. Using a cheese grater or food processor, grate the potato, and place in a bowl of cold water; let sit for about 10 minutes

2. Preheat your Cuisinart waffle maker.

3. Add a 1/2 cup potato in the center of a tea towel, one at a time, twist and squeeze to remove as much water as possible; repeat until all potato is drained.

4. Brush each side of the waffle iron with some butter using a silicone basting brush. Pack the potato shreds in the center of the waffle maker. Sprinkle with salt and pepper to taste.

5. Close the waffle maker lid. Set the timer for 8 to 10 minutes. Flip the waffle maker over.

6. When the time has expired and the waffled hash browns are golden brown—they are done.

7. Using a thin spatula, gently transfer your hash brown to a serving plate. Top as desired and serve immediately.

Nutritional Info: Calories: 167 | Sodium: 172| Dietary Fiber: 1.9 g | Total Fat: 11.6 g | Total Carbs: 14.9 g | Protein: 1.9 g.

Waffled Jalapeno Hashbrown

Servings: 2 | Prep Time: 10 minutes | Cook Time: 10 - 20 minutes

Kick things up a notch with these delicious Waffled Jalapeno Hashbrowns! Full of spice and clean eating ingredients, these waffles are the perfect comfort snack or side dish for days when you feel like being a little naughty with your diet.

Ingredients

2 russet potatoes, peeled and grated

1 jalapeño, diced

1/8 teaspoon sea salt

1/2 tablespoon olive oil

Instructions

1. Preheat the waffle maker.

2. Place the grated potatoes in a potato ricer to squeeze out the excess liquid. **Note: Alternatively, you can use doubled up cheese cloth or paper towels, but this is crucial to the cooking process.

3. Toss together the potatoes, jalapeño, olive oil and salt in a bowl.

4. Pile all of the potatoes onto the waffle maker.

5. Close the waffle maker lid. Set the timer for 5 minutes, grasp both handles and flip the waffle maker over 180°.

6. Cook for 10 - 20 minutes or until to desired crispness and serve.

Nutritional Info: Calories: 183 | Sodium: 131| Dietary Fiber: 5.8 g | Total Fat: 3.8 g | Total Carbs: 35.1 g | Protein: 3.9 g.

Waffled Kimchi Fried Rice

Servings: 2 -4 | Prep Time: 55 minutes | Cook Time: 10 minutes

Whip up some delicious, savory fried rice right in your Cuisinart Belgian Waffle Maker. These delicious waffles are perfect for lunch, dinner or brunch - especially when they are topped with a farm fresh fried egg.

Ingredients

1 teaspoon olive oil

1 cup kimchi centers, chopped

1/4 cup kimchi juice

3 cloves of garlic, minced

1/2 small onion, finely chopped

1/2 jalapeño pepper, finely chopped

1 tablespoon gochujang/Korean chili paste

3 teaspoons sesame oil

2 cups white rice, cooked and refrigerated

Sesame seed, for topping

Fried egg, for topping

Instructions

1. Add olive oil and garlic to a medium frying pan. Fry until fragrant.

2. Add onions and jalapeño and fry for 2 additional minutes.

3. Add kimchi and sauté for 2 to 3 minutes, until softened. Next, add the gochujang and mix well.

4. Fold the cold rice into the frying pan and break it up thoroughly.

5. Drizzle in the kimchi juice and sauté, tossing frequently, for 5 mins. Add sesame oil and stir well.

6. Remove from heat; let it cool in the refrigerator for 45 minutes to keep waffles from falling apart.

7. Preheat the waffle maker.

8.   Add 1 cup of batter to the waffle maker.

9.   Close the waffle maker lid. Set the timer for 4 minutes. Flip the waffle maker over.

10.   Remove the waffled polenta from iron with a spatula or fork and top with a fried egg. Sprinkle with sesame seeds and enjoy!

Nutritional Info: Calories: 420 | Sodium: 490| Dietary Fiber: 1.8 g | Total Fat: 5.9 g | Total Carbs: 80.4 g | Protein: 7.2 g.

Waffled Polenta

Servings: 4 servings | Prep Time: 10 minutes | Cook Time: 10 minutes

Polenta is the perfect substitute for bread, pasta or potatoes as it perfectly takes on the robust flavors it's combined with. Great as a main meal or side dish, this Italian corn meal treat fits with any clean eating, gluten-free and paleo meal plan.

Ingredients

1 (18-ounce sleeve) pre-cooked polenta

1/4 teaspoon sea salt

1/4 teaspoon black pepper, coarsely ground

2 teaspoons olive oil

1 cup cherry or grape tomatoes, halved

1 1/2 cups zucchini, sliced and halved

Non-stick cooking spray

Parmesan cheese, shaved for topping

Instructions

1. Preheat the waffle maker and set the oven to warm.

2. Heat a frying pan on medium heat and add 1 teaspoon of olive oil.

3. Add tomatoes and zucchini. Sprinkle with salt and pepper, and sauté while you waffle the polenta stirring often.

4. Spray each side of the waffle maker griddle with a thin layer of cooking spray.

5. Place slices of polenta on the waffle maker.

6. Close the waffle maker lid. Set the timer for 4 minutes. Flip the waffle maker over.

7.   Remove the waffled polenta from iron with a spatula or fork, and transfer to a baking sheet. Place the polenta waffles into the warm oven while you cook the other polenta rounds.

8.   Add two polenta waffles to each plate. Remove the sautéed zucchini and tomatoes from the stove top. Top waffles equally with vegetables, garnish with shaved parmesan and a drizzle of the remaining olive oil to serve!

Nutritional Info: Calories: 512 | Sodium: 126| Dietary Fiber: 4.4 g | Total Fat: 3.6 g | Total Carbs: 108.6 g | Protein: 10.5 g.

Zucchini Waffles

Servings: 4 | Prep Time: 10 minutes | Cook Time: 10 minutes

Ditch the pasta and rice sides, and cook up something decadently different for dinner. Zucchini waffles are just one more amazing way to pack your meal with something super tasty.

Ingredients

2 medium zucchini, spiralized or shredded

1 large egg

1/4 cup kefir or almond milk

1/2 cup parmesan cheese, grated

1/2 cup almond flour

Nonstick cooking spray

1 teaspoon sea salt

1/4 teaspoon black pepper

Pizza sauce, for dipping

Instructions

1. Place the spiralized zucchini in a colander and sprinkle with 1/4 teaspoon salt.

2. Let the salted zucchini sit for about 30 minutes. Then rinse well with cold water and press out as much of the water as possible. Squeeze dry with paper towels.

3. Preheat the waffle maker.

4. Whisk together the egg, milk, and 1/4 cup of the grated Parmesan in a large mixing bowl.

5. Combine the flour with the other 1/4 teaspoon salt and 1/4 teaspoon freshly ground black pepper in a large mixing bowl.

6. Fold the contents of the small mixing bowl into the large mixing bowl.

7. Add the zucchini and toss until everything is well-combined.

8. Coat both sides of the waffle maker griddle with nonstick spray.

9. Place one rounded tablespoons of the batter into each quarter of the waffle maker; leave room for the waffles to spread slightly.

10. Cook about 3-5 minutes or until light golden. Repeat with remaining waffle batter.

11. Serve topped with the remaining 1/4 cup parmesan and pizza sauce for dipping.

Nutritional Info: Calories: 160 | Sodium: 761| Dietary Fiber: 1.4 g | Total Fat: 11.1 g | Total Carbs: 5.3 g | Protein: 12.2 g.

11

Kid-Friendly Waffles

Brownie-Sundae Waffles

Servings: 4 | Prep Time: 15 minutes | Cook Time: 20 minutes

Mini-Chefs will love preparing their very own homemade sundaes. While we love traditional sundae toppings, don't be afraid to get creative and top it with anything you want!

Ingredients

3/4 cups all-purpose flour

2 tablespoons unsweetened cocoa powder

1/8 teaspoon sea salt

4 ounces bittersweet or semisweet chocolate, chopped

3 tablespoons unsalted butter, plus more for brushing waffle maker

1/2 cup sugar

2 large eggs, beaten

Vanilla ice cream, for topping

Whipped cream for topping

Caramel sauce, for topping

Sprinkles, for topping

Maraschino cherries, for topping

Instructions

1. Sift together the flour, cocoa powder and 1/8 teaspoon salt in a medium mixing bowl and set aside.

2. Combine half the chocolate and the butter in a medium saucepan over medium heat, for about 5 minutes. Stir until melted and smooth.

3. Remove from chocolate mix from heat and let cool slightly.

4. Fold in the sugar and eggs. Add the flour mixture and remaining chocolate and stir until just combined.

5.   Lightly brush the top and bottom of the waffle maker with butter.

6.   Fill the waffle maker about three-quarters of the way full with batter.

7.   Close the waffle maker lid. Set the timer for 4 - 6 minutes. Flip the waffle maker over.

8.   Cook until the waffles are cooked through and slightly crispy around the edges.

9.   Transfer waffles to a plate and keep warm with tented aluminum while you cook the remaining waffles.

10.   Top each waffle with a scoop of ice cream, caramel sauce, whipped cream, sprinkles and a cherry—and enjoy!

Nutritional Info: Calories: 449 | Sodium: 178 | Dietary Fiber: 2.5 g | Total Fat: 20.1 g | Total Carbs: 61.4 g | Protein: 8.4 g.

Pizza Waffles

Servings: 2 | Prep Time: 10 minutes | Cook Time: 10 minutes

Turn pizza night into something spectacular with your Cuisinart Belgian Waffle Maker. Mini-chefs will love creating their very own pizza to enjoy, so don't be afraid to go overboard with the toppings.

Ingredients

1 can ready-made pizza crust, like Pillsbury

1 (15-ounce) can of pizza sauce

2 cups mozzarella cheese, shredded

1/2 teaspoon oregano

1/2 teaspoon garlic powder

1/4-pound sandwich pepperoni

1/4 cup green peppers

Non-stick cooking spray

Instructions

1. Preheat the waffle maker.

2. Roll the ready-made pizza crust out onto parchment paper. Cut into four squares to fit your waffle maker.

3. Spread a few tablespoons of pizza sauce onto two pieces of the pizza crust. Top with a layer of mozzarella cheese.

4. Add an even layer of pepperoni and green peppers. Finish with a second, even layer of mozzarella.

5. Lay one extra square of plain crust on top of each pizza.

6. Spray both sides of the Cuisinart waffle maker with non-stick cooking spray.

7. Lay one pizza into the waffle maker.

8. Cook for 3-4 minutes or until golden and crispy. Remove and repeat with the second pizza.

9.   Serve piping hot with extra pizza sauce for dipping!

Nutritional Info: Calories: 1130 | Sodium: 1048 | Dietary Fiber: 4.5 g | Total Fat: 67.4 g | Total Carbs: 49.6 g | Protein: 83.2 g.

S'moreffles

Servings: 4 | Prep Time: 2 hours 15 minutes | Cook Time: 15 minutes

Give the kids something fun to do on a Friday night in with the Cuisinart Belgian Waffle Maker! They'll feel just like they're round the campfire without leaving the comfort of home.

Ingredients

2 cups unbleached flour

1 cup dark brown sugar

1 teaspoon baking soda

3/4 teaspoons sea salt

7 tablespoons unsalted butter, cut into pieces, chilled

1/3 cup honey

5 tablespoons whole milk

2 tablespoons pure vanilla extract

Pinch of cinnamon

For the S'more Filling:

2 bars dark or milk chocolate broken, into pieces

1 jar marshmallow fluff

Instructions

1. Mix the dry ingredients in a mixing bowl.
2. In a separate bowl, whisk the milk, honey and vanilla until well-blended.
3. Add the butter to the dry ingredients and rub together with your hands until the mixture looks like coarse cornmeal.
4. Add the milk mixture to the flour mixture until a dough forms.

5. Wrap in plastic wrap and place in the refrigerator to chill for at least two hours, or overnight.

6. Lightly flour a work surface.

7. Roll out the dough with a rolling pin so that it is just over a quarter of an inch thick. Cut out the dough into 4 inch squares.

8. Preheat and grease the Cuisinart Belgian Waffle Maker with non-stick cooking spray.

9. Place one square into each quarter of the Cuisinart waffle maker.

10. Cook 3 - 4 minutes or until crisp.

11. Set aside the waffled graham crackers and continue to cook until all batter is use.

12. To assemble the s'moreffles, spread marshmallow fluff onto each waffled graham cracker. Place a few pieces of chocolate into the center of the cracker.

13. Place one waffled graham cracker. Close the lid and heat for one minute each. Serve warm and enjoy.

Nutritional Info: Calories: 925 | Sodium: 885 | Dietary Fiber: 2.5 g | Total Fat: 27.4 g | Total Carbs: 159.1 g | Protein: 9.3 g.

Waffle Cake

Servings: 6 - 8 | Prep Time: 15 minutes | Cook Time: 15 minutes

Go hog wild with this super fun recipe! Kids will love mixing up their favorite fun filled cake batter and turning it into delicious waffles topped with all kinds of decadence like ice cream and hot chocolate sauce.

Ingredients

1 box funfetti cake mix

1 cup water

1/3 cup vegetable oil

3 eggs

Non-stick cooking spray

Instructions

1. Whisk together the cake mix, water, oil, and eggs in a large mixing bowl until well combined.

2. Drop 2 1/2 ice cream scoops of the cake batter into the Cuisinart waffle maker.

3. Cook for 2 -3 minutes or until golden and fluffy. Repeat for remaining cake batter.

4. Serve warm with a scoop of ice cream and a drizzle of chocolate syrup.

Nutritional Info: Calories: 383 | Sodium: 459 | Dietary Fiber: 0.6 g | Total Fat: 17.9 g | Total Carbs: 51.2 g | Protein: 5.0 g.

Waffle Dogs

Servings: 6 - 8 | Prep Time: 15 minutes | Cook Time: 15 minutes

Mini-chefs will love these yummy little hot dogs they can help adult chefs make at home. Try serving them up with tater tots and some carrot sticks—and don't forget the ketchup and mustard for dipping fun!

Ingredients

8 nitrate-free hot dogs

8 slices whole grain bread

Waffle batter, [*See Belgian Waffle Recipe on page 58**]

3 tablespoons honey

16 wooden toothpicks

Non-stick cooking spray

Instructions

1. Use a rolling pin to flatten out the bread slices as much as possible. Roll each hot dog up in a slice of flattened bread.

2. Secure each edge of bread with a toothpick, placed about 3' apart, by piercing sideways through the hotdog.

3. Whisk the honey into the waffle batter.

4. Use tongs to dip and coat three bread wrapped hot dogs in the batter and place onto the waffle iron.

5. Cook for 5 minutes or until golden brown.

6. Repeat with the remaining hotdogs. Remove all of the toothpicks and serve your waffle dogs with your favorite dipping sauce.

Nutritional Info: Calories: 925 | Sodium: 185 | Dietary Fiber: 2.0 g | Total Fat: 9.0 g | Total Carbs: 19.0 g | Protein: 8.5 g.

Waffled Cookies

Servings: 20 | Prep Time: 15 minutes | Cook Time: 20 minutes

Load your waffle maker with cookie dough for one seriously amazing dessert. Everyone will love these delicious chocolate chunk cookies - especially when you get the kids involved in this quick, easy treat.

Ingredients

1/2 cup packed brown sugar

1/4 cup granulated sugar

1/2 cup butter

1 egg

1 teaspoon pure vanilla extract

1 cup and 2 tablespoons all-purpose flour

1/2 teaspoon salt

1/4 teaspoon baking soda

1/2 cup dark chocolate bar, chopped into chunks

Non-stick cooking spray

Instructions

1. Melt the butter in a microwave safe bowl.
2. Pour it into a large mixing bowl and add both sugars. Stir together until smooth.
3. Add egg and vanilla and stir again until well-blended.
4. In a separate mixing bowl, whisk together the flour, soda and salt.
5. Add chocolate chunks to dry ingredients and stir.
6. Fold the dry ingredients into the large mixing bowl and mix well, but do not over stir.
7. Place the cookie dough into the refrigerator and preheat the Cuisinart Belgian Waffle Maker.
8. Scoop one teaspoon into each of the four griddles. Close the waffle maker lid and flip the waffle maker.

9. Lift the lid to check on the cookies, you can bake them for another 30 seconds if you want them more brown and crunchy.

10. Remove and set cool on a wire rack. Serve with a tall glass of milk or almond milk and enjoy.

Nutritional Info: Calories: 116 | Sodium: 115 | Dietary Fiber: 0.0 g | Total Fat: 6.1 g | Total Carbs: 14.0 g | Protein: 1.4 g.

12

Bonus: Pantry

What to Have On Hand for Cuisinart Belgian Waffle Maker

Sauces & Syrups

Sauces and syrups are a great way to top waffles. Don't be afraid to mix and match sauces and syrups for tantalizing flavor combinations for endless ways to change up your favorite waffle recipe.

- Butter
- Syrup
- Liqueurs
- Melted butter and Maple Syrup
- Melted butter and honey
- Caramel sauce
- Nutella
- Peanut Butter
- Marmalade
- Lemon curd
- Homemade jam
- Jelly or preserves
- Yogurt
- Chocolate pudding
- Fudge sauce
- Honey
- Chocolate sauce
- Powdered Sugar
- Ice Cream
- Caramelized Bananas
- Strawberries & Cream
- Whipped cream with sprinkles
- Cinnamon Roll Icing
- Rum
- Vanilla Extract
- Orange flower water

Candies and Sweets

Your favorite candies and sweets make for one delicious way to top your homemade waffles. Don't be afraid to get creative with your waffle creations.

- Chocolate chips
- Butterscotch chips

- Peanut butter chips
- Malted milk balls
- Whipped cream
- Peppermint Pattie pieces

- Sugar
- Powdered sugar
- Brown sugar
- Pearl sugar
- Crushed candy bars

Fruit

Fruit makes for a healthy and nutritious way to top your amazing waffles!

- Bananas
- Strawberries
- Apples
- Blueberries
- Raspberries
- Cherries

- Mangos
- Peaches
- Pineapples
- Kiwis
- Passion fruit
- Berry compote

Nuts

Get nutty with your waffles and add delicious nuts and seeds for a healthy alternative to sweet toppings.

- Almond
- Australian Nut
- Beech
- Black Walnut
- Blanched Almond
- Brazil Nut
- Butternut
- Candle Nut
- Candlenut

- Cashew
- Chestnuts
- Chinese Almond
- Chinese Chestnut
- Chinkapin
- Chufa Nut
- Cobnut
- Colocynth
- Country Walnut

- Cream Nut
- Cucurbita Ficifolia
- Earth Almond
- Earth Nut
- English Walnuts
- Filbert
- Florida Almond
- Gevuina Avellana
- Gingko Nut
- Hazelnut
- Heartnut
- Hickory Nut
- Horned Water Chestnut
- Indian Beech
- Indian Nut
- Japanese Walnut
- Java Almond
- Jesuit Nut
- Juniper Berry
- Kluwak Nuts
- Kola Nut
- Macadamia
- Malabar Chestnut
- Mamoncillo
- Maya Nut
- Mongongo
- Oak Acorns
- Ogbono Nut
- Para Nut
- Paradise Nut
- Pecan
- Persian Walnuts
- Pili Nut
- Pine Nut
- Pine Nut
- Pinyon
- Pistachio Nut
- Pistacia
- Polynesian Chestnut
- Queensland Nut
- Royal Walnuts
- Rush Nut
- Sapucaia Nut
- Shagbark Hickory
- Sliced Almonds
- Slivered Almond
- Sweet Almond
- Sweet Chestnut
- Terminalia Catappa
- Tiger Nut
- Walnut
- Water Caltrop
- White Nut
- White Walnut
- Chia seeds
- Flaxseed
- Hemp seeds
- Poppy seed
- Pumpkin seeds

- Sesame seeds
- Safflower
- Sunflower

Savory Toppings

Waffles don't have to be sweet, they can be just as delicious with savory toppings too!

- Ham & Cheese
- Blue cheese crumbles
- Parmesan cheese and oregano
- Feta cheese
- Country gravy
- Cheddar and green chili

Types of Non-Dairy Alternative, Gluten-Free & Paleo Friendly

Toppings

No matter which way you like you waffles, savory and sweet alike, these toppings are great for healthy living lifestyles.

- Lemon juice and powdered sugar
- Marshmallows
- Sorbet
- Raisins
- Cinnamon
- Cinnamon & sugar
- Garlic powder & butter
- Fried egg
- Scrambled egg
- Chili
- Buffalo chicken
- Cinnamon apple sauce
- Coconut milk
- Strawberries & Cream
- Pumpkin puree
- Fried chicken
- Salsa

Next Steps...

DID YOU ENJOY THE BOOK?

IF SO, THEN LET ME KNOW BY LEAVING A REVIEW ON AMAZON! Reviews are the lifeblood of independent authors. I would appreciate even a few words and rating if that's all you have time for. Here's the link:

http://www.healthyhappyfoodie.org/z3-freebooks

IF YOU DID NOT LIKE THIS BOOK, THEN PLEASE TELL ME! Email me at feedback@HHFpress.com and let me know what you didn't like! Perhaps I can change it. In today's world a book doesn't have to be stagnant, it can improve with time and feedback from readers like you. You can impact this book, and I welcome your feedback. Help make this book better for everyone!

DO YOU LIKE FREE BOOKS?

Every month we release a new book, and we offer it to our current readers first...absolutely free! This helps us get early feedback before launching a book, and lets you stock your shelf full of interesting and valuable books for free!

Some recent titles include:

- The Complete Vegetable Spiralizer Cookbook
- My Lodge Cast Iron Skillet Cookbook
- 101 The New Crepes Cookbook

To receive this month's free book, just go to

http://www.healthyhappyfoodie.org/z3-freebooks

Made in the USA
Middletown, DE
14 December 2018